TRUE CRIME FLORIDA

The State's Most Notorious Criminal Cases

Catherine Cole & Cynthia Young

STACKPOLE BOOKS

0 11557 03628 2

Published by
STACKPOLE BOOKS
5067 Ritter Road
Mechanicsburg, PA 17055
www.stackpolebooks.com

Printed in the United States of America

10 9 8 7 6 5 4 3 2 1

FIRST EDITION

Cover design by Tessa J. Sweigert

Cover Photos: Clockwise from top left, Palm Beach County sheriff Robert Baker; Ted Bundy in state custody, 1978; Ashley Gang member Roy Young Matthews; Ashley gang member Handford Mobley. All photos courtesy Florida Photographic Collection, State Library and Archives of Florida. Image of handcuffs and badge, ©Photosani/Shutterstock.

Library of Congress Cataloging-in-Publication Data
Lower, Catherine.
  True crime, Florida : the state's most notorious criminal cases / Catherine Cole and Cynthia Young. — 1st ed.
      p. cm.
  Includes bibliographical references.
  ISBN-13: 978-0-8117-3628-2 (pbk.)
  ISBN-10: 0-8117-3628-8 (pbk.)
  1. Criminals—Florida—Case studies. 2. Murder—Florida—Case studies. 3. Crime—Florida—Case studies. I. Thuma, Cynthia. II. Title.
  HV6793.F6L69 2011
  364.109759—dc22
                                              2011001393

Contents

INTRODUCTION

As our license plates proclaim, Florida is the Sunshine State. The image the state and its citizens like to nurture is that of a sun-splashed, family-friendly place where the sun and the beaches attract visitors from all over the globe. As a result, Florida is one of the world's great tourist destinations. But for nearly every moment of light, there is darkness; in the evening the sun sets and creatures of the night emerge. Some of the crimes chronicled in this book occurred at night, some during the daytime. A few, such as the murders of Curtis and Marjorie Chillingworth and of Mary Dene Harvey and four members of the Arthur Duperrault family, occurred at sea.

The CQ Press's annual compilation of state crime statistics has shown Florida to have one of the nation's highest instances of crimes per 100,000 people. In 2008, Florida had the ninth-highest crime rate; the state shot to fourth in 2009 and eased back to fifth in 2010, behind Nevada, New Mexico, Louisiana, South Carolina, and Tennessee.

The state's law enforcement agencies are working hard to apprehend and punish the offenders. According to Florida Department of Law Enforcement statistics for 2008–09, more than one million arrests were made for crimes against people and property.

The stories selected for this book span the last century, from 1911, when John Ashley shot and killed Indian trapper DeSoto Tiger, to 2003, when Palm Beach millionaire Fred Keller shot his wife, Rosemarie, and his brother-in-law, Wolfgang Keil. (Rosemarie Keller died, but Wolfgang Keil survived.) We not only recount the crimes, we also trace what has happened in the wake of each crime. In a many cases, surviving family members and others have taken action to strengthen Florida's laws, better track offenders, assist social service and law enforcement agencies, and make other significant changes to prevent additional crimes.

CHAPTER 1

1911: The Ashley Gang

In Arthur Penn's 1967 film *Bonnie and Clyde,* the heinous image of Bonnie Parker and Clyde Barrow's gang was buffed up and glamorized for the big screen. The Florida-based Ashley gang had a movie made about it, too, one not nearly as well known: *Little Laura and Big John.* This film, written and directed by Luke Moberly, was released in 1973 and starred Karen Black and Fabian. It was a bit less ambitious than *Bonnie and Clyde* and not nearly as critically acclaimed. Still, despite their differing fame in film, the careers of both groups of criminals were equally heinous and depraved.

Julius W. "Joe" Ashley (1861–1924), his wife Lugenia Clay Ashley (1862–1946), and their five sons moved from the Fort Myers area to Pompano Beach in 1904. In 1911, they moved again, first to West Palm Beach and then farther north to the small community of Gomez, in what is now Martin County, not far north of the Palm Beach County line. The oldest son was Julius "Ed" Ashley, born in 1880 (died 1921); he was followed by William Sidney, better known as Bill (1883–1940); John Hopkins (1888–1924); Franklin "Frank" Zetlis (1900–21); and Robert Harris, better known as Bob (1894–1915). There also were two daughters: Daisy May (1904–28), who, during her adulthood, lived in the Jacksonville area, and Bertha A. (1889–1931). Joe Ashley worked on the railroad as a wood chipper, served as a Palm Beach County deputy sheriff, and did other odd jobs to make ends meet for his large family, but it wasn't long before he turned to moonshining, a fairly common occupation for the time and location.

John, the family's middle son, was by most early accounts a model child—polite, well-behaved, and hardworking. John Ashley seemed particularly at home in the dense scrub of palmetto, scrubby oak, and shortleaf pine that covered much of south Florida. He was an excellent hunter and an adept trapper, but he was particularly admired for his skill as a marksman. Where most shooters would stand cans and bottles up along a ledge or rail for target practice, John Ashley would place them on their sides, shoot through the holes, and blow the bottoms out.

John spent a significant amount of time working his traps in the area around Lake Okeechobee. Sometimes he hunted and trapped with Seminoles who lived around the lake. Shortly after Christmas in 1911, a dredging crew found the lifeless body of DeSoto Tiger, son of a local Seminole chief, in a gator hole in northwestern Dade County. Tiger had been shot in the back and dumped in the hole. His cache of pelts was nowhere to be found. Two other Seminoles who had accompanied him on his last day, Gopher Tiger and Girtman Billy, told police the last person they had seen with Tiger was John Ashley—who later sold a load of eighty otter pelts to J. D. Girtman in Miami for $584. Once Palm Beach County sheriff George Bell Baker learned of Tiger's death, he dispatched a pair of deputies to question Ashley. As the deputies approached the family's home, John and Bob leaped from the surrounding brush with guns drawn, startling the deputies. They chided them for their ineptitude and sent them back to Sheriff Baker with a message: send better, more stouthearted officers next time.

Ashley went on the run after the deputies' visit. For two years, law enforcement officers searched for John Ashley without luck. He was reported to have fled to the New Orleans and Seattle areas, and other reports placed him in Canada. It was homesickness that brought him back to Florida, where he turned himself in to Palm Beach County authorities in 1914.

Ashley admitted he had shot Tiger, who, he said, had threatened to shoot him first. Ashley's testimony was a roll of the dice. He had reasoned that jurors were more likely to believe the words of a white man over an Indian, particularly in a case with little evidence and no witnesses to the crime. He was nearly right. The trial ended in a hung jury, split 9–5 in favor of acquittal. The retrial was scheduled for Dade County, and Palm Beach County deputy Robert C. Baker, Sheriff Baker's son, was assigned to transport Ashley back to Palm Beach County. Because of Ashley's gentle demeanor and cooperative attitude, Deputy Baker decided not to cuff him for transport. As they left, Ashley saw an opportunity arise and he took it, running from Baker, scaling a high fence, and disappearing.

John's family closed ranks and rallied behind the fugitive, and as a result, the Ashley gang began to form. The first gang activity was probably a February 1915 train robbery attempt that went badly awry. A porter, alerted by a passenger's screams, locked down the cars so John Ashley, his father Joe, nephew Handford Mobley, and a family friend were isolated from the other cars and passengers. The robbers fled from the train near Gomez, where the Ashley family still made its home. Sheriff Baker couldn't find John Ashley, but he did pick up Joe, Mobley, and the friend. No prosecutions came from the incident, but the Ashley gang was gradually building its reputation.

Near the end of February, John and Bob Ashley, aided by a Chicago thug named Kid Lowe, held up the Bank of Stuart, taking about $4,500. As the three departed the bank, Lowe fired a few shots to keep potential pursuers and the curious at bay, but one of the shots struck John Ashley in the right jaw. The slug deflected upward, hitting Ashley's left eye and blinding it. The injury made it easy to take Ashley into custody, but the others got away.

Ashley was again sent to Dade County's jail. The family sent word that he would be leaving there well before authorities saw fit to release him. As a result, the jail's security was beefed up.

On June 2, 1915, Bob Ashley calmly pedaled a bicycle to the jail. He walked to the home of Deputy Wilber W. Hendrickson, forty-four, who lived next door. He knocked; Hendrickson came to the door.

"You Hendrickson?" Ashley asked. The deputy nodded, and before he could say anything, Ashley shot him. Immediately, chaos reigned. Hendrickson's wife screamed, grabbed a rifle, and started after Ashley. Ashley, who was searching the deputy's body, looking for the master jail key, panicked. He found the key, but dropped it in panic as he fled. He commandeered a passing car, and when its driver wasn't driving fast enough to suit his needs, Ashley took the wheel. Two Miami police officers caught up with the vehicle a few blocks from the jail. Officer John Rhinehart "Bob" Riblet, walking his beat, spotted the vehicle and ordered Ashley to step from the car. Ashley refused and fired, hitting Riblet in the mouth. Though injured, Riblet squeezed off a pair of shots, hitting Ashley with both. Both men succumbed to their injuries. Riblet, thirty-one, was the first Miami police officer to die in the line of duty.

After the failed breakout, John Ashley's murder charge for the death of DeSoto Tiger was dismissed, but the state's very strong case against him for the Stuart bank robbery went forward, with Ashley pleading guilty. He was sentenced to seventeen years at the Raiford State Penitentiary. Again, Ashley proved to be a model prisoner and, as such, was assigned to a road crew in March 1918. Three months later, he and another prisoner simply strolled away from the crew. Ashley's girlfriend Laura Upthegrove, who was conveniently waiting a few blocks away, gave the two men a ride back home.

A tall, dark-haired, rawboned woman who often wore a .38 strapped to her right leg, Upthegrove, like her boyfriend, was comfortable in the swamp and scrub surroundings. She grew up at Upthegrove Beach, a tiny town on the north shore of Lake Okeechobee that was founded by her father and his two brothers. She had been married twice and was the mother of three before she and John Ashley became an item. Hardly the gun moll she is sometimes portrayed as, she gave the gang a lookout, an organizer, and someone who kept an eagle eye on the books and the enterprise's product. She was sometimes dispatched to scout out potential robbery sites. Quite simply, John and Laura completed each other; together they were the power couple of Florida's underworld. Alone, John Ashley was "The Swamp Bandit," but together they were the "King and Queen of the Everglades."

Laura Upthegrove was a woman of contradictions. She was the dark lamb of the Upthegrove family, which otherwise established a reputation of distinction and public service in South Florida. Her uncle Robert Upthegrove filed the papers to establish the Upthegrove Beach settlement in 1912 and served on the Okeechobee County Commission, as did his son Harvey. Laura's brother, Clarence DeWitt Upthegrove, served as supervisor of elections in Palm Beach County from 1944 to 1961. Other members of the Upthegrove family ran for public positions (some successfully, others not) and continue in public service to the present.

As the Ashley and Upthegrove families had deep roots in South Florida, so did the Baker family. Sheriff George Baker died on March 8, 1920, and Robert Baker, who had become his father's deputy at age twenty-one in 1909, was sworn in as his successor. Robert Baker was a gritty, determined police officer who had lost a foot a year after becoming a deputy when a prisoner in his custody managed to grab a gun and squeeze off a shot. Baker eventually needed to have his leg amputated as a result of the injury. Already bitter, the animosity Robert Baker felt for the Ashley gang had been brewing for years and already was intense by the time he became Palm Beach County's top lawman. Baker had trusted Ashley at the Dade County jail, and Ashley gave him the slip. Baker might also have been one of the deputies dispatched to question Ashley after De-Soto Tiger's body was found, though we don't know for sure.

Prohibition began in 1920, providing plenty of opportunities for the gang to provide powerful, illegal spirits to thirsty consumers, especially aided by patriarch Joe Ashley's expertise. The Ashley gang saw income potential and entered the moonshining and rum-running businesses with gusto. Joining them were Ed and Frank Ashley, their nephew Handford Mobley, Roy "Young" Matthews, and Upthegrove. The gang worked the moonshining venture from several angles, from operating three stills in Palm Beach County and at least one in Martin County, to double-crossing rumrunners in the Bahamas and participating in piracy on the high seas. Moonshining was a high-risk, high-reward enterprise, and the Ashley gang members proved themselves uncommonly adept and successful at it. Multiple vehicles were needed to deliver the 'shine, so gang members found themselves constantly stealing "fresh" vehicles to use. At least one local judge had a vehicle stolen by the gang.

Their efforts also took a grim toll on the gang. Ed and Frank Ashley disappeared at sea in December 1921. John was apprehended while delivering moonshine in Wauchula, in Hardee County, and was returned to Raiford. He escaped in 1923, and the gang hit banks in Homestead and Pompano shortly thereafter. The robbery of the Bank of Pompano was particularly successful, netting $5,000 in cash and $18,000 in securities. Gang members whooped it up and hollered as they sped away.

In February 1924, the gang again turned its attention south to the city of Pompano (now Pompano Beach). Joe Tracy, a latecomer to the gang, rented a taxi and had the driver take him and several gang members to Deerfield Beach, where the remaining gang members waited. They commandeered the cab and tied the cabbie to a tree with a gift—a bullet for Sheriff Baker. John Ashley told the cabbie to present the bullet to the sheriff personally with a message from them: "We'll see you in the Everglades."

John Ashley's arrogance had been a continual source of embarrassment and irritation to Sheriff Baker. The bullets Ashley had victims from robbery sites deliver to him were a source of humiliation and anger. The sheriff had vowed to Ashley he'd wear the Swamp Bandit's glass eye on his watch chain someday. He had promised to bring the Ashley gang down, but had little to show for it so far.

In the wee hours of January 9, 1924, Baker led a posse outside the Ashley moonshine camp at Fruita, near Hobe Sound. At first light, the posse, led by Deputy Frederick A. Baker and composed of Ernest Malphurs, J. G. Padgett, H. L. Stubbs, and Sim Jackson, moved in and opened fire. Joe Ashley was killed in the skirmish. John Ashley saw who took the shot that dropped his father. He braced his rifle against a tree and gunned down Deputy Baker, the third lawman to die at the hand of gang members, and the third Palm Beach County police officer to be killed in the line of duty. The skirmish had taken away John Ashley's father, and Deputy Baker was Sheriff Baker's cousin; the tensions between the Ashley gang and the Bakers was escalated another notch, just under full boil.

Local citizens had finally had enough, too. In the years prior to the shootout, the gang had cultivated a Robin Hood–like image. Gang members never robbed or stole from women and there were ample local legends of good deeds done and uncommon compassion shown by the gang members to members of the community who were down on their luck or suffering. As time passed, however, even the staunchest local support waned. Locals were especially enraged by the murder of Deputy Baker and the gang's continued influence in the area. They formed a posse and burned the camp where the shooting had taken place, as well as the Ashley and Mobley homes.

While the gang's base of operations may have been destroyed, their lawbreaking ways continued. The teenaged Handford Mobley orchestrated one of the gang's most famous capers—the second robbery of the Bank of Stuart in September 1924. In it, Mobley, who was tall and slender, dressed in women's clothing, complete with high heels, floppy hat, and handbag. Once inside the bank, he took off the hat, pulled out a gun, and announced his intentions. He ran outside with the take—where Matthews and John Clarence Middleton waited—and took off.

Not long after the Stuart bank heist, the end came swiftly for the Ashley gang. The longstanding feud between Sheriff Baker and John Ashley had reached its crescendo. By October 1924, Baker's officers had ferreted out all the Ashley stills and hideouts and destroyed them.

Ashley had every intention of killing Sheriff Baker, but wanted to first lie low for a bit. Doing so would allow him to raise some additional capital through bank robberies and plot his future moves. He had decided to go to north Florida for a while, apparently planning to visit his sister Daisy as part of the trip. Law enforcement had been tipped off about the gang's plans and route, possibly by Laura Upthegrove, who was peeved she hadn't been invited to go along with Ashley, Handford Mobley, Clarence Middleton, and Ray "Shorty" Lynn. This would be the gang's final trip.

On the evening of November 1, 1924, at the Sebastian River bridge on Dixie Highway about thirty miles north of Fort Pierce, deputies strung a chain across the road and hung a lantern from it. St. Lucie County Sheriff James R. Merritt and two deputies, J. M. Smith and Ollie E. "Three Fingers" Wiggins, crouched in the bushes near the chained-off bridge, swatting at insects and making small talk as they waited. Sheriff Baker had contacted Merritt and told what he'd learned of the gang's plans. He dispatched deputies Elmer Padgett, Oren B. Padgett, Henry Stubbs, and Lem B. Thomas to assist Merritt. The lawmen met at the bridge, hid their vehicles, and waited patiently until well after nightfall.

The gang members had taken their time moving up the coast, amusing themselves by playing pool and visiting a barbershop along the way. With new haircuts and smooth-shaved faces, they resumed their journey north. Finally, shortly before 11 P.M., their black touring car slowed to a stop behind another car at the entry to the bridge.

The first car to stop contained two young men who lived in the area, Ted Miller and S. O. Davis. Officers told the lads to move along, and as they prepared to drive away, another car pulled up. Miller and David watched the flood of officers rush from hiding and surround the vehicle. In it were the four members of the Ashley gang, with Handford Mobley at the wheel and John in the backseat. Resting near John's hands was a small arsenal that included a Winchester 25/35 rifle, a pearl-handled revolver, and a pair of Thompson submachine guns.

The officers had truly surprised the gang members, who didn't have time to draw their weapons. The officers pulled the car's doors open and yelled at Ashley and his companions, ordering them to step from the vehicle, raise their hands, and not move otherwise. Ashley was separated from his cohorts, and deputies swiftly began cuffing the men.

Sheriff Merritt saw that Miller and Davis still hadn't left the area and were gawking at what was happening behind them. Thinking the deputies had the situation firmly in control, Merritt approached them and told them he and his men had just taken the Ashley gang into custody. He even showed them the pearl-handled revolver he'd taken from John. Merritt asked the young men if he could step onto their running board and get a lift to the other side of the bridge, where he had parked his car. They said yes.

Just as Merritt began the short ride to the other side of the bridge, a barrage of gunshots rang out. The specifics have long been murky and the accounts riddled with contradictions, but the basic facts were simple: At least one of the Ashley gang members made a move the posse members considered threatening, and the shooting began. Seconds later, four dead bodies lay on the ground and the Ashley gang's reign of terror was over.

Miller and Davis testified that when they last saw the gang members, they were standing alongside the road in handcuffs, hands raised above their heads. They testified at a coroner's inquest that the gang members had to have been shot while handcuffed. A second coroner's inquest featured testimony by Sheriff Merritt and the deputies at the scene, who disputed the testimony of Miller and Davis, saying the gang members were not handcuffed at the time of the shooting. The unanimous verdict in the second proceeding was justifiable homicide.

The Ashley gang is dead and gone, but never quite forgotten. The old Bank of Stuart building—the site of the second Stuart robbery—long served as a restaurant called the Ashley, which was filled with Ashley memorabilia and photos. The Ashley opened in 1990 and featured the bank's original tile floor, brickwork, and ornate ceiling. A portion of a wooden teller booth was incorporated into the interior design. The restaurant, a shrine to all things Ashley, closed in 2006; it was later revived under different management but closed for good in 2009.

John Ashley—along with most of the rest of his family—slumbers in a tiny family cemetery on what are now the grounds of the Mariner Sands Country Club in Stuart. Joe and Lugenia Ashley are buried there, as are their sons Bob and John, as well as Bill, who declined to join in the criminal activities. Their daughters Daisy and Bertha are there as well. The small, tidy cemetery also contains a dual headstone commemorating their sons Ed and Frank, who died at sea; their nephew Handford Mobley and gang member Ray Lynn are buried there, too. Clarence Middleton, the fourth member of the Ashley gang killed at the Sebastian bridge, was taken by family members for burial in north Florida. After the shooting on the Sebastian River bridge, Laura Upthegrove was treated as a pariah by the family. She died in 1927 at the age of 30, after drinking a bottle of disinfectant during a fit of anger at her family's service station at Canal Point.

The family cemetery is ringed by vegetation John Ashley would have found comforting: scrub oak, palmetto, and a few shortleaf pine trees. The cemetery is wedged in between the upscale development's chapel and the eighteenth tee of its golf course. Each year, the golf club remembers the Ashley gang with a tournament in their honor—The Ashley Shootout.

CHAPTER 2

1955: The Chillingworth Murders

Curtis Eugene Chillingworth and Joseph Alexander Peel Jr. were alike in several ways. Both men were West Palm Beach natives and members of prominent, well-respected families who went on to become attorneys, and then judges.

Chillingworth's father was Charles C. Chillingworth, who had served as West Palm Beach's first city attorney. His grandfather had been a mayor of West Palm Beach. Peel's father was Buck Peel, a West Palm Beach hotel owner.

Peel earned his law degree at Stetson University's College of Law, Florida's first law school. Chillingworth, a member of the first graduating class of Palm Beach High School, graduated at the head of his class at the University of Florida's law school. In 1920, when he was twenty-four, Curtis Chillingworth was elected county judge for Palm Beach County, making him the youngest judge in the state.

For twenty-five days in 1947, Judge Peel became Associate Justice Peel, substituting for Florida Supreme Court Justice Harold Sebring, who had been appointed to the U.S. Military War Crimes Tribunal in Nuremberg, Germany.

At the time their lives collided, Joe Peel and Curtis Chillingworth were both married and were fathers.

In every other respect, the two men were polar opposites. Judge Chillingworth was a jurist of impeccable credentials with a spotless record of service to his nation in the military, his profession, and his community. He married Marjorie M. McKinley, a gentle, sweet woman who had attended Cornell University and loved gardening, particularly raising Gerbera daisies. Together, they became parents of three daughters: Ann, Marie, and Neva. Humorless and a bit priggish when in his black robes and in his chambers, Judge Chillingworth aimed for the highest and best for himself. In his thirty-four years on the bench, very few of his rulings were overturned or modified. He set lofty goals for himself and his performance, and usually hit the mark.

Judge Peel aimed far lower and hit the mark with regularity, too. As the municipal judge in West Palm Beach, Peel cut a handsome, almost dashing appearance, favoring white linen suits and tooling around town in a Cadillac. Beneath his flashy appearance ran a darker vein. Peel ran a protection racket for bolita, bootlegging, and other illegal activities. Ironically, a local Jaycees club once named him "man of the year." Peel married Imogene Clark, from Lake City, a beauty who had held the title of "Miss Stetson" while in college. Just after Peel graduated from law school, they started their family in Palm Beach County, where Peel opened his law practice in 1949.

Virtually from the start, Peel played fast and loose in the courtroom, and Judge Chillingworth was usually there when he stumbled. Peel's first ethical misstep came in 1952, when he urged a client to lie in court. In 1953, Judge Chillingworth learned Peel had represented both the plaintiff and defendant in a divorce. He reprimanded Peel and warned him that further ethical lapses would force him to remove him from the bench and consider starting disbarment proceedings.

In 1955, Peel informed a female client that her divorce was final when in fact, it wasn't. The woman remarried and the new couple gave birth to a child before the woman learned that she had become a bigamist through Peel's inaction. Her case was set to go before Judge Chillingworth for disposition, and word had reached Peel that the judge intended to deal with him harshly. Peel feared for the worst and began hatching a plan. He petitioned the court for a delay and located an old acquaintance, Floyd Albert Holzapfel, better known by his nickname, "Lucky." Holzapfel had proved himself an expert in helping Peel tidy up the messes in his life, particularly when it required a little persuasion to get the job done, and Peel had called on him with relative frequency. After a shady adolescence, which included bookmaking and a pair of armed robbery convictions, Holzapfel seemed to have straightened himself out. He built a distinguished military record, and then became a police fingerprint expert in Oklahoma City, but his life gradually spiraled downhill again. By 1955, he was working as a mechanic in West Palm Beach.

Holzapfel enlisted the help of George David "Bobby" Lincoln, a brawny man who owned several pool halls north of West Palm Beach. Peel fed him a well-edited version of what needed to be done and why. Judge Chillingworth, he told them, represented a threat to their underworld interests and had to be dealt with. He had to go.

Judge Chillingworth was feeling the weight of his community on his shoulders. He was a punctual, precise, and efficient man and over the course of more than three decades on the bench, he had heard thousands of cases, issued thousands of rulings, and affected thousands of lives. Finally, he had decided to retire and had drafted his letter of resignation, but had not yet turned it in to Gov. LeRoy Collins. Outside the courthouse, Chillingworth had invested wisely in real estate and he and his wife had every reason to look forward to a comfortable retirement. But they never got the chance.

Sometime in the wee hours of June 14, 1955, or the early ones of June 15, Judge Chillingworth answered a knock on the door of his beachfront home in Manalapan. When the judge opened the door, Holzapfel and Lincoln burst in and subdued him and his wife. Chillingworth offered the intruders money, but they refused. At gunpoint, they forced the couple across the beach to the water's edge. There a small boat awaited them, pushed onto the sand. Holzapfel ordered the Chillingworths to get in. They cast off and rode in the inky darkness for a while, accompanied by the purr of the small motor. Finally, Holzapfel told Lincoln to cut the motor and ordered Marjorie Chillingworth to stand. The men bound her with chains and weights and Holzapfel gestured toward the water with his gun.

"Ladies first," he said.

Chillingworth looked into his wife's eyes and spoke evenly. "Remember," he told her. "I love you."

"I love you too," she said, just as she was pushed from the boat.

Judge Chillingworth was next. He was a strong swimmer and, despite the chains and other weights, wouldn't sink. He kept thrashing, trying to get away. Holzapfel finally hit him in the head with the butt of his shotgun. The blow was so forceful the wood splintered, but the judge still struggled to stay afloat. Holzapfel and Lincoln tossed a loop of the rope attached to the boat's anchor around the judge's neck and threw the anchor in the water. The judge sank beneath the surface of the water. Holzapfel threw the shotgun in behind him. Suddenly it was silent and peaceful off the coast of Palm Beach. Holzapfel and Lincoln rode back to land and Holzapfel called Peel.

"The motor is fixed," he told him. The terse message was code; it meant the deed had been completed.

The next day, a pair of carpenters found no one at home when they arrived for work at the Chillingworth house. They'd been dispatched there to fix a broken window frame and do some other work around the house. At the same time, at the county courthouse, Judge Chillingworth was late for a 10 A.M. hearing—and Judge Chillingworth, normally as punctual as a Swiss watch, was never late. When Sheriff John Kirk was notified, he dispatched deputies immediately, but feared the worst. A massive search was begun. Clues were few:

Some droplets of blood were found on the steps leading out to the beach, along with two empty adhesive tape rolls and footprints in the sand. When investigators checked the home, they found money in the judge's wallet and his wife's purse and the couple's Plymouth in the driveway. The lack of evidence—and lack of bodies—kept investigators from making meaningful progress on the case.

By 1957, the case had gone cold and the Chillingworths were declared dead. It languished another year until an investigation into another killing yielded some surprising leads. An agent from the Florida Sheriff's Bureau, Henry Lovern, had been hanging out among the state's moonshiners trying to get leads on the 1958 murder of bootlegger Lew Gene Harvey when he met Jim Yenzer, an insurance agent with ties to the underworld. Yenzer said he knew nothing about the Harvey murder—which had been another of Holfzapfel and Lincoln's jobs—but he did know a little, he said, about the disappearance of a judge and his wife. Lovern feigned indifference, but could barely conceal his enthusiasm to learn more. Yenzer wanted to be helpful, and as the scraps of information dribbled in, Lovern began to see the case take shape. Yenzer eventually began working as an intermediary between Lovern, Holzapfel, and Peel, although neither Peel nor Holzapfel knew Yenzer was working with anyone but them. Yenzer's helpful attitude was understandable, perhaps, because there was reward money to be made if the Chillingworth killers were caught.

Yenzer worked so hard to gain Holzapfel's confidence that he participated in several criminal activities with Holzapfel. In one of those capers, a hijacking, Holzapfel was arrested.

Lovern worked carefully to collect evidence and learn the facts of the judge's death, and the motivations of the man who ordered the killings. In December 1959, Holzapfel bolted unexpectedly, later turning up broke in Rio de Janeiro. He'd been trying to contact Joe Peel for money and Peel was not as responsive as he'd hoped. Peel was beginning to regard Holzapfel as a pest and Holzapfel's anger with Peel was growing.

Peel wasn't responding to his requests for money, and Holzapfel was feeling indignant. Peel, for his part, was feeling apprehensive and decided the best way to take care of his anxiety and uncertainty was to remove the cause. So he called Yenzer and asked him to kill Holzapfel.

Lovern and his fellow lawmen worked out a double-cross scenario to lure Holzapfel back to the United States and arrest him and Peel for the murders of the Chillingworths. It all unfolded in the Melbourne area, in motels along the beach. Holzapfel returned from abroad and contacted Peel, who in turn contacted Yenzer. He told Yenzer he wanted the hit carried out as quickly as possible. Yenzer alerted Lovern and then called Peel, asking him to come to his motel room. He told him he had a special message for him.

Holzapfel showed up at Yenzer's room. Yenzer welcomed him in and motioned toward a table. He placed two glasses on the table and opened a bottle of whiskey. The men sat down and talked. They talked for the greater part of three days. Yenzer told him of the contract Peel had on him and finally, Holzapfel had heard enough: He'd served Peel so well for so long, and this was the thanks he got for it? He began to recount the details of the Chillingworth murders.

Yenzer called Peel and told him he'd carried out the contract. As they spoke, Lovern and members of the Brevard County Sheriff's Office broke into the room, guns drawn. Holzapfel looked at them warily and stood up, raising his hands. He was inebriated as well as tired, emotionally and physically. Once he got to the jail, Holzapfel attempted suicide by slitting his wrists, but was too drunk and fatigued to carry it out.

Peel was arrested a few days later. His reaction was unlike Holzapfel's; he was calm, cool and cagey. He tried to make a deal to gain immunity, and promised to implicate Holzapfel and Lincoln. State Attorney Phil O'Connell laughed at him.

On March 7, 1961, Peel went to trial for the murder of the Chillingworths; his legal woes blossomed elsewhere as well. On June 16 of that year, he and several others, Holzapfel among them, were indicted for fraud in the sale of securities of Insured Capital Corporation. But Peel had more trouble than he could handle at the Chillingworth trial, which was held in Fort Pierce, two counties north of Palm Beach. O'Connell didn't have the bodies or much forensic evidence, but Holzapfel and Lincoln testified, and that was enough to earn Peel's conviction as accessory after the fact.

Bobby Lincoln, at that time in federal prison for his moonshining activities, asked for and received immunity for the murders of Lew Gene Harvey and the Chillingworths, in exchange for his testimony. Lincoln was released from prison in 1962. He moved to Chicago and converted to Islam, changing his name to David Karrim. He died in May 2004, at eighty years of age.

Despite his nickname, Floyd Holzapfel was not so lucky. He hadn't asked for immunity or any other kind of a deal before he talked. After his trial—which, ironically, was held in Judge Chillingworth's old courtroom, with a large portrait of the judge seemingly scowling at him from the wall—he was sentenced to death for his role in the Chillingworth murder. The sentence was later commuted to life, and he died in prison in 1996.

Joe Peel lived long enough to gain parole, but not by much. At the time of his release, his body was racked with colon, liver, and lung cancer. After his release, he admitted for the first time his role in the deaths of the Chillingworths. He died nine days after he was set free.

Joe and Imogene Peel divorced and Imogene married Al Cone, founder of a West Palm Beach law firm that had earned a reputation for nurturing its young lawyers into some of the state's best jurists. Al Cone served as a role model to A. Clark Cone, Joe and Imogene's son, who also became an attorney. A. Clark Cone was disbarred in 2009 after being charged with cheating clients out of more than $600,000.

The bodies of Curtis and Marjorie Chillingworth were never found, but their names and legacy live on. In 2000, Curtis and Marjorie Chillingworth's daughters Neva Chillingworth, Ann C. Wright, and Marie C. Cooper, along with son-in-law Bill Cooper, started the Judge Curtis E. and Mrs. Marjorie M. Chillingworth Memorial Scholarship Fund at Florida State University, the Chillingworth daughters' alma mater. The fund provides scholarships annually to assist bright, talented students in their quest to become teachers.

CHAPTER 3

1961: The *Bluebelle* Tragedy

When the sixty-foot ketch *Bluebelle* eased out of Fort Lauderdale's Bahia Mar marina bound for the Bahamas on November 8, 1961, hardly anyone noticed. A large, bustling marina, Bahia Mar sees heavy charter vessel traffic every day of the week and season of the year. Boats come and go throughout the day and even at night, whether setting out for a day's fishing, cruising the shoreline, or departing for an island cruise.

Aboard this particular ketch was the Duperrault family of Green Bay, Wisconsin. The father, Dr. Arthur Duperrault, was a hardworking, kind, and generous optometrist. He was seriously weighing moving his family to Florida, where they could sail all year and avoid the long, frigid Wisconsin winters. Dr. Duperrault was a man highly invested in the lives of his wife and children, as well as the vitality of his community. He volunteered at the elementary school,

19

the local chapter of the YMCA, and elsewhere. Dr. Duperrault's wife Jean was a dark-eyed, dark-haired beauty who had a penchant for Asian art and decorating. Together, Arthur and Jean Duperrault had three children: Brian, age fourteen; Terry Jo, age ten; and Renee, who was seven.

Guiding the boat was Julian Harvey, forty-four, and his wife, Mary Dene Harvey, thirty-eight, a former flight attendant, who acted as the vessel's cook. Harvey was a handsome man who worked hard to cultivate his dashing image. He was a retired lieutenant colonel in the U.S. Air Force, and had served as a test pilot. But he had done more, too. He had been a male model and was a serious bodybuilder, working out compulsively. No one loved Julian Harvey as much as Julian Harvey.

The first few days of the cruise were exactly what they were supposed to be—a sun-splashed dream vacation, with carefree days of fishing, snorkeling, and swimming in the beautiful azure waters. There, seabirds swooped around the vacationers, screeching and diving. Flying fish and playful dolphins also came near the boat. The family made one stop on land, at Sandy Point on Great Abaco Island. Every member of the Duperrault family was having the time of his or her life.

Then, in the dark of the last evening of the cruise, the nightmare began.

According to Captain Harvey, during the night of November 12, the *Bluebelle* was engulfed in a sudden strong squall that snapped the boat's mast. The broken mast crashed to the deck, piercing it and the hull and separating Harvey from his wife and the passengers. Terry Jo, he said, was screaming, but everyone else was calm, despite the deteriorating conditions. Water was pouring into the boat and a fire, caused by ruptured fuel lines, broke out and spread quickly as the sails became engulfed in flames. Harvey said he released the boat's dinghy and life raft and called to the others to abandon ship. He then dove off the *Bluebelle* for the dinghy, hoping to rescue the others, but only found the body of little Renee, floating facedown. No matter how long or hard he looked, Harvey said he could find no further trace of his wife or the rest of the Duperrault family. For more than two hours, he said, he paddled about, calling out for Mary Dene and the Duperraults, but only heard silence in the darkness.

The next morning, Harvey was picked up by a passing ship, the *Gulf Lion*. He had Renee's body with him; he had lashed her body to the boat. The crew radioed the Coast Guard in Miami and dropped him off in Nassau.

Four days after the sinking of the *Bluebelle*, a lookout on the bridge of the Greek freighter *Captain Theo* spotted a small patch of white in the waters off the Bahamas. The white patch remained in place, as if it were painted on the water. Normally, the whitecaps expose themselves, fold over, and disappear, but the white patch he was watching was unwavering. The sailor pointed the spot out to his captain, who ordered that they go closer to find out what it was. As the ship drew closer, sailors gathered on the starboard side of the boat, near the bow. The patch of white was a young girl, perched oddly on the side of a raft. The sailors brought the girl aboard and tended to her until a helicopter was dispatched to take her to Miami. As she was lifted to the helicopter in a basket, she raised a weak, sunburned hand to wave goodbye to the men who had plucked her from the sea and cared for her.

At that same time in Miami, just after Harvey completed his testimony before a Coast Guard inquiry, the hearing was interrupted to announce that after four days adrift, Terry Jo Duperrault had been found alive on the *Bluebelle*'s raft. She had been taken to the city's Mercy Hospital unconscious and horribly sunburned. Her chances of survival were iffy, but she was alive and there was hope. When he heard the news, the color drained from Harvey's face.

"Oh my God," Harvey said. "That's wonderful." So great was his joy, he said, he needed a moment to get a sip of water and compose himself. He excused himself from the hearing room, bypassed the restroom, and headed for his room at the Sandman Motel on Biscayne Boulevard in downtown Miami. There he sat down and began to write. After completing his note, he pulled out a double-edged razor and with it slashed as deeply as he could into his left thigh, his wrists, his ankles, and his neck. He had placed pictures of his son Lance and Mary Dene, the wife who had gone down with the *Bluebelle,* in front of him, apparently to look at in his last minutes.

Several hours after Harvey left the hearing room, a maid rapped on his door at the motel. She had come to Room 17 to make the bed and tidy up. When she got no answer, she opened the door with her pass key. When she went to clean the bathroom, the door was unlocked but wouldn't open. She brought her supervisor, who could not move the door either. He called for a police officer, who managed to force the door and saw the body of Julian Harvey, dead on the floor in a pool of blood. Then they found the two-page suicide note in an envelope on the desk.

Coast Guard investigators, like the public, were puzzled. By then, the story of the *Bluebelle*'s tragic final voyage had been splashed across the front page of newspapers across the nation and world. The picture of the unconscious Terry Jo, her face and lips grossly swollen, was heating the wires up again. Captain Harvey's suicide made no sense to most, but his friends believed it was the final act of a man whose nerves simply wore out after one adventure too many. Harvey had survived two plane crashes as an Air Force pilot, and a bridge crash that killed his third wife and her mother. He had survived when two of the boats he captained sank. The latest incident and the apparent deaths of his wife and the four members of the Duperrault family were simply the last straw, his friends theorized.

Terry Jo spent two days in a coma. Several days passed before she regained full consciousness, but then her condition rapidly began to improve. Finally her doctors agreed to let her talk with Coast Guard officers investigating the *Bluebelle*'s demise. The story she told them differed from Harvey's in almost every detail.

✳ ✳ ✳

On the night of the *Bluebelle*'s sinking, screams and pounding noises had awakened Terry Jo. She recognized the voice of her brother, screaming for their father. Then she heard more noises, but no more screaming, and after a few minutes, no noise at all. She waited a few more minutes for good measure, and then crept into the main cabin of the boat, where she found the bodies of her mother and brother lying on their backs next to each other in a pool of blood. A look at their faces told her they were both dead. Elsewhere on the boat, she found another pool of blood, but no more bodies. Finally, she came upon Harvey. Before she could ask what had happened, he hit her and shoved her down the stairs, telling her to go back to her room.

Terry Jo did as she was told, climbed back into bed, and tried to understand was going on. Harvey strode into her room, holding what appeared to be a rifle, but after staring at her for a moment, he turned and left without having said a word. After a while, she noticed water had begun climbing up the wall in her room. The water continued to rise steadily and by the time it reached the level of her waist, she realized she had to go on deck or she'd drown.

Once on deck, she encountered Harvey again and asked if the boat was sinking. He said yes, and then handed her the rope to the ketch's dinghy and told her to hang onto it. Numb and in shock from what she'd witnessed, Terry Jo didn't react as the rope slipped from her fingers and the dinghy drifted off. She continually looked for her father and her little sister, but saw neither of them and heard nothing except the noises Harvey was making and the sound of her own heart.

Harvey returned and yelped when he saw Terry Jo. The dinghy was drifting away, he said. He dove overboard and that was the last she saw of him. She found the boat's raft, untied it, climbed aboard, and shoved off. It was a clear, quiet evening. There had been no squall, no broken mast, and no fire. It had been a night of murder, plain and simple.

The Coast Guard learned that in the months before the last cruise of the *Bluebelle,* Harvey had purchased a $20,000 life insurance policy on his wife that would pay double if she died an accidental death. Harvey was the policy's sole beneficiary.

In February 1962, the U.S. Coast Guard's report on the *Bluebelle* tragedy ruled that the ketch was intentionally scuttled and sunk by Julian Harvey after he killed his wife and four members of the Duperrault family. The report listed five circumstances that made Terry Jo's survival possible. It concluded Harvey did not harm Terry Jo or Renee because he assumed they'd drown when the boat sank. Renee donned a life jacket but drowned anyway. Harvey, the report's authors surmised, kept Renee's body to add credibility to his story.

In the months following her rescue, Terry Jo was swamped with gifts, prayers, and good wishes from dignitaries and common people around the world. President John Kennedy sent a note; Pope John XXIII sent a rosary. The crew members of the *Captain Theo* pooled their funds and sent her a giant doll.

After Terry Jo recovered from the ordeal, she returned to Wisconsin to live with family members. She changed her first name to Tere, married several times, and became a parent and then a grandparent. She is now retired from a career as a water management specialist with the Wisconsin Department of Natural Resources.

In 2010, a book written by her and psychologist Richard Logan entitled *Alone: Orphaned on the Ocean* was released by TitleTown Publishing. In an interview with Matt Lauer on *The Today Show,* Tere said she wrote the book in the hope of benefiting others.

"I thought that I was spared for a reason, and the reason would be to help other people," she told him.

In the wake of the *Bluebelle* tragedy, one lasting change has benefited mariners cast adrift on the waves. The specifications for the appearance of lifeboats, life rafts, and buoyant floats were changed in February 1962. The new specifications mandated that the color of these flotation devices be changed to international orange to increase visibility.

CHAPTER 4

1968: The Mackle Kidnapping

Being buried alive may be one of humankind's most primal fears. And in the past, it was not too uncommon. History is pockmarked with cases of people who, for one reason or another, were buried a bit prematurely. In most instances, the victims were not conscious at the time of burial and therefore not aware of the hell that awaited them. Unfortunately for Barbara Mackle, she was.

The Emory University student was not feeling well just before Christmas break in 1968. The Hong Kong flu was raging across the country and had struck with a vengeance on the Atlanta campus. Barbara called home to tell her mother, Jane, that she was ill but intended to stick it out and finish her final exams before flying home to Coral Gables, Florida. Jane Mackle decided she would fly to Barbara and help nurse her through the illness. Her intention was to remove Barbara from classes and get her the medical attention she needed, knowing that the local hospitals and medical clinics would be overrun with those suffering from the same illness. Jane thought she, a healthy adult, would be better able to navigate the health care situation than her poor, sick daughter.

The two women checked into the Rodeway Inn at the edge of the Emory campus in Decatur, Georgia, on December 13. Fortunately, under her mother's tender loving care and with some much-needed medications, Barbara was able to study and return to campus to take her exams. After the exams were over, mother and daughter would travel back home together for the holidays. All was going according to Jane's plan. But her plan did not mesh with someone else's—someone who wanted something Jane possessed.

At 4 A.M. on Tuesday, December 17, the two women were startled awake by a knock at their door. When they answered, the man outside claimed he was a police officer and told them Barbara's fiancé had been hurt in a car accident. When Jane opened the door, what appeared to be two men wearing ski masks burst in with an assault rifle. Jane was bound and overcome with chloroform. They easily overpowered the still-recovering Barbara and snatched her from the room. She was wearing only a flannel nightgown in the frigid north Georgia night.

The kidnappers drove Barbara twenty miles farther north, to a remote location near Duluth, Georgia. The driver turned off the highway and drove into a patch of woods, taking the car off-road about 100 feet through the trees. He removed the limbs that had been hiding a coffin-shaped and sized capsule. It was then that Barbara first got a glimpse of her hell on earth.

The capsule, constructed of plywood and lined with fiberglass, was about three feet wide, three-and-a-half feet deep, and seven feet long. While the driver pried the top off the capsule, he regaled Barbara with all he had done to keep her safe until the ransom was paid. The capsule had enough food for a few days, sedative-laced water, a fan to move air about, a lamp to keep the darkness at bay, and a blanket and sweater for warmth. Two plastic pipes the kidnapper had installed would allow air from the surface to fill the underground coffin.

As her fate sunk in, Barbara begged her kidnappers not to bury her. But that was part of their "perfect" plan. The kidnappers used chloroform to subdue her so she was drowsy but not unconscious when they lowered her into the capsule. She cried out time after time as they screwed down the lid and filled in the grave with hundreds of pounds of clay and dirt. They camouflaged the area with branches and tree limbs so that to the casual observer, the area would seem undisturbed. Mackle later said in a book she coauthored about her ordeal that she listened through the air tubes as the shoveling gradually stopped, footsteps moved away from the area, and the car was started and driven away.

Panic was threatening to overtake her, because she was trapped below ground with zero chance to free herself. After the sound of the motor faded away, Mackle ordered herself to calm down. Her breathing was ragged and her chest was heaving. She needed to assess the situation. It was then that she found a typed note from her kidnappers that proudly laid out the details of the capsule.

"Do not be alarmed. You are safe. You'll be home for Christmas one way or the other," the note began. It then listed the amenities of the capsule, which included a battery-operated fan and light that it said would remain operational for a full eleven days. That, however, was wrong. In less than three hours, the battery was dead. Barbara Mackle wondered what else they had gotten wrong and whether she would soon be just as dead as the battery,

She spent the next three days in an underground hell. Barbara had no idea what was going on above her or a state away in her native Florida. She had no way of knowing that her father had paid the half-million-dollar ransom, and that her kidnappers had used a pay phone to call the FBI with directions to where she was buried alive.

Agents raced to Duluth. The first agents on the scene spoke to Barbara through the air tubes, and then began clawing at the earth with their bare hands to try to reach her more quickly. FBI Agent Ange Robbe told the *Atlanta Journal-Constitution* that Mackle kept saying, "Please don't leave me." The agents assured her they would not leave her until she was out of her tomb. She was finally freed eighty-three hours after she was first buried—stiff, dehydrated, and weighing about ten pounds less than when her ordeal began.

She immediately flew back to Miami on her father's private plane and met briefly with the press. She insisted that she felt wonderful and told everyone her kidnappers had treated her humanely—as humanely as possible when one is buried underground for more than three days. Her plan was to put this behind her and get on with her life. But the FBI was not going to let this fade away like the nightmare it was. The FBI agents had not yet gotten their man, and they were not going to rest until they did. Fortunately, the man they were chasing—the self-proclaimed "Einstein of crime"—was as faulty as the capsule he had devised, and he led the authorities right to himself.

Gary Steven Krist was a petty criminal who had been planning his big score since he was fourteen years old. He had mainly been involved in small-time robberies (at least that was what was believed at the time) in his native Alaska and Utah, where he had been raised. But he had an idea, one that he spent years plotting and scheming. Finally, in the fall of 1968, the time seemed right for the twenty-three-year-old Krist. He began to put his plans into action. Krist started by searching the Miami area for the perfect victim for his perfect crime. He spent weeks poring over the *Miami Herald*, other local newspapers, and the social register to find his target. He first narrowed his list to one hundred potential victims, all female, and then spent days eliminating them one by one. As he carefully considered each, he found one reason or another that she was not the "perfect" victim.

Finally, a single name remained—Barbara Jane Mackle. Her father, Robert Mackle, co-owned the Deltona Corporation, one of the first developers of planned communities in South Florida, with his two brothers, Elliott and Frank Jr. Their father, Frank Mackle Sr., had developed Key Biscayne as affordable housing for soldiers returning from World War II. The $10,000 ranch-style houses soon became known as "Mackles," and their style was unmistakable: low to the ground, with thick walls, and constructed out of hurricane-resistant concrete block. They sold incredibly well to veterans home from the war and eager to realize the American dream. His sons replicated his success in various areas around Florida, including Deltona, Spring Hill, St. Augustine Shores, and Marco Island.

They were put on the proverbial and literal map, though, when Richard Nixon bought a Mackle on Key Biscayne and often hosted distinguished guests from the world of politics. His Senate colleague George Smathers visited often while Nixon was still in office. It became the "Winter White House" and was the location where plans for the now infamous Watergate break-in were discussed. The Winter White House was actually part of a compound that included several homes, a private beach, and a $400,000 floating helipad for Marine One that was built by the U.S. Department of Defense. It was also the place where Nixon retreated during the height of the scandal that eventually engulfed his presidency. His close friend and confidant Charles "Bebe" Rebozo lived next door.

The home was razed in 2004 to make way for a bigger home for its current owners. Back in its day, though, it served a president. And that president and Robert Mackle were soon friends and publicity followed . . . publicity Robert probably soon came to regret, because that high profile was the reason Krist found Barbara. And once he found her, he was going to use her to make himself a wealthy man.

Krist, though his methodical research, learned that Mackle and his family lived in Coral Gables, a prestigious and wealthy community just south of Miami. Robert and his wife, Jane, had two children, Robert Jr., age twenty-four, and Barbara, twenty. When Krist discovered that Mackle's firm was worth about $65 million, the tall, attractive co-ed was soon the focus of all of his research and planning. Krist wanted $500,000, and Barbara seemed the most expedient way to get it. The goal was the ransom payoff; Barbara was just a means to an end. Krist had been planning this crime—according to later prison records—since he was a young teenager.

The only way Krist could pull off the kidnapping was with the help of a partner. Ruth Eisemann, a native Honduran, graduated from National University of Mexico and was a graduate student at the University of Miami's Institute of Marine Science when she met Krist. She bought into his plan to kidnap the brunette and eagerly did what she could to help.

After doing his research and selecting Barbara as his target, Krist built the underground capsule in a trailer at the University of Miami. He spent hours on the construction and special modifications necessary to keep Barbara alive until the ransom was paid. When it was ready, he loaded it into a Volvo station wagon and drove it twelve hours north. He and Eisemann located a remote spot in the piney woods outside Atlanta and spent the better part of a day digging a hole in the hard clay in which to bury the capsule. They were fairly confident that the area was not one in which someone might accidentally find the capsule holding Mackle. They left soon after digging the hole and concealing it with branches and brush.

They arrived in the Atlanta area the same day as Jane Mackle. But whereas Jane had come to town to help her daughter, Krist and Eisemann had other plans. But first they had to find her. Posing as a scholarship investigator, Krist learned the name of Barbara Mackle's dorm just by inquiring at the admissions office. Today's Family Educational Rights and Privacy Act (FERPA) laws would never allow that to happen. Colleges and universities are prevented from disclosing any information about a student to anyone—even a parent—without express written consent from the student. But this was another time, and people readily offered information. Another resident in the dorm told Krist that the recuperating Barbara was staying with her mother at the Rodeway Inn just off campus. It did not take him long to discover which room was theirs, and he soon made his move.

After leaving the terrified and panicking Barbara in the capsule, Krist and Eisemann returned to the Miami area to carry out the plans for the $500,000 ransom drop. Krist had already determined that the best way to collect the money was to call the Mackle residence with his demands and instructions for the drop. If the family agreed to the ransom demands, Krist instructed them, they were to place an ad in the next day's newspaper.

The following morning, a small ad appeared in the classified section in which the family, using a carefully worded code devised by Krist, made it very clear they would pay any amount for the return of their daughter. This was just what Krist and Eisemann had been waiting for—now they could put the rest of their plan into action. Later that night, Krist phoned the Mackle home with instructions for the drop. Robert was to leave the money on a seawall along the Fair Isles Causeway at Biscayne Bay, just a few miles from the Mackle mansion in Coral Gables. Fair Isles was uninhabited, with little chance of the kidnappers being observed.

The plan called for Krist to wait in a boat nearby until the drop was made. At that point, he would go ashore, gather the ransom, and make his way to the Volvo, where Eisemann was ready at the wheel. It was a good plan, and it might have worked had Krist not lost his way in the dark. As the kidnapper picked up the suitcase nearly an hour later than had been planned, a police officer saw him and thought he was a burglar. The officer gave chase on foot. Eisemann abandoned the Volvo, inadvertently leaving behind a great deal of pertinent information about the kidnappers: passports, checkbooks, documents with past addresses, a collection of women's undergarments, nude Polaroids of both Krist and Eisemann . . . and a Polaroid of Barbara Mackle holding a sign that said, "Kidnapped." It was not the brightest of ideas to keep all of these items in the getaway car, and now Krist and Eisemann had to deal with the fact that the authorities more than likely knew who they were.

They decided their chances were better if they separated, so they planned to rendezvous in Austin, Texas, and then make their way to

Europe. Eisemann boarded a bus heading west, while Krist remained local to plan the second ransom drop. He phoned the Mackle home at 10:35 P.M. and demanded a new drop on Southwest Eighth Street. This time the ransom was paid without incident, and Krist finally had his half million dollars. But his wealth was short-lived. By the time the second ransom was paid, the FBI did indeed know the identity of both kidnappers and was already making plans to catch them.

Warrants were issued and both Krist and Eisemann were placed on the FBI's Ten Most Wanted list, but the FBI really did not have much of an idea about where to find either of the kidnappers . . . that is, until the "Einstein of crime" made a mistake. Krist thought his best route for escape would be by water. He planned to cross Florida via its extensive canals, and then cross the Gulf of Mexico to Texas, where he would meet up with Eisemann. But first he needed a boat.

The morning after the crime, Krist purchased a sixteen-foot motorboat at D&D Marine Supply in West Palm Beach. He used the name Arthur Horowitz and paid for the boat in $20 bills—all $2,240 of the purchase price. Not exactly an inconspicuous transaction for a man who was supposed to be keeping a low profile as he made his somewhat lengthy and drawn-out escape. By this time, the Mackle kidnapping was front-page news all across America, and the story went into great detail about how the ransom had been paid in $20 bills to a big, burly, bearded man. At D&D Marine, owner Norman Oliphant found it suspicious that this big, burly, bearded man had paid for the boat from a thick stack of $20 bills, and he called the police just after "Arthur Horowitz" left. Oliphant's quick thinking and willingness to help aided the police and the FBI as they tracked the most wanted man in America. Now they had a starting place for their hunt.

Krist was a hunted man. The night of December 20, 1968, he made his way across Florida through a series of locks on the Florida Intracoastal Waterway. Each lock had a tender whose job it was to record the names, types, and destinations of vessels passing through. When the lock tenders each questioned him about the lack of registration for the boat, he simply told each one that he had lost it. He nearly made it, too. But the tender at the final lock before the Caloosahatchee River in Fort Myers became suspicious of Krist and his story and radioed his colleagues across the state. He soon learned Krist has used the same story at the first lock near St. Lucie and all the way across the state. He let Krist through but called the authorities, who quickly determined it was the kidnapper. They came at Krist from the air, water, and land. He went ashore on Hog Island, a thirty-square-mile island off Fort Myers, where he took off on foot. After nearly twelve hours of running and hiding, Krist was finally captured.

The authorities recovered all but the cost of the boat and $761 from Krist's "perfect crime." His partner, Ruth Eisemann, was arrested two days later after applying for a job in Norman, Oklahoma. She was extradited to Georgia to stand trial, where she was found guilty and sentenced to seven years in prison. After just four years, she was paroled and deported to her native Honduras. She remains persona non grata in the United States.

While in custody awaiting his own trial, Krist apparently wanted to have his criminal mind recognized as far superior to those of the common deviants with whom he now found himself consorting, and he confessed to three murders and alluded to a fourth. He killed his first victim when he was just fourteen, he said, a sixty-five-year-old man with whom he had had a homosexual relationship in Pelican, Alaska. He said he had killed the man by tripping him while they were walking across a bridge over a deep ravine. The cause of death at the time was listed as an accident. The second murder, Krist said, took place just four years later. He claimed that he had killed a girl near San Diego, strangling and beating her to death before hiding her body under rocks. The body of Helen Crow had been found on October 3, 1964, and the coroner had placed her time of death at six to eight weeks prior. However, at the time of her murder, Krist was in prison in Tracy, California. No one really knows how he had such detailed knowledge of the crime or the crime scene. The third homicide Krist confessed to took place just after he had escaped from jail in Utah. He said he had picked up a homosexual and killed him in a fit of rage, dumping the body near Wendover, Utah. A skeleton was discovered there on July 12, 1967, and the estimated time of death was three to five years earlier—a time that coincided with the timeline of Krist's criminal activity or lack thereof. He also alluded to a fourth homicide but remained closemouthed about the details. Krist, it seemed, talked when he wanted about what he wanted. Investigators were at his mercy.

But so was he at theirs. They had done their homework and had the facts ready when the trial for the kidnapping of Barbara Mackle began. Krist was literally fighting for his life as the prosecutor, Richard Bell, sought the death penalty for the cruel and unusual kidnapping. Krist was found guilty but was instead given a life sentence. Krist was diagnosed as borderline schizophrenic by a prison psychiatrist and seemed to believe, despite his capture and conviction, that his plan had been brilliant and failed only because he had made a slight miscalculation about the number of authorities chasing him on Hog Island. Even sitting in his cell, he truly believed his plan had been incredibly well thought out, planned, and executed.

Not that he wanted to be sitting in that cell for long. He tried desperately to get out—even contacting his victim for help. In 1971, he wrote a letter to Barbara Mackle and asked for her forgiveness. He told her he knew his crime was evil, immoral, inexcusable, and undeserving of forgiveness. He would, however, be very grateful to receive it from her, and he would learn from his crime and move on. When that did not work, he decided instead to try to woo the public and published a memoir in 1972, titled *Life: The Man Who Kidnapped Barbara Mackle*. It failed miserably at its goal—the public held little sympathy for the man who had buried his victim alive. He eventually tried to escape from prison but was discovered hiding in a garbage truck.

He remained in prison until his release in 1979, at the age of thirty-three. He had made good use of his time behind bars and began to tutor fellow inmates and take college classes. He trained as an emergency medical technician and worked in the prison hospital. He even befriended James T. "Tommy" Morris, the chair of the Georgia Parole Board. He was eligible to apply for parole after serving just seven years of his sentence. Morris convinced the rest of the parole board that Krist was not a danger to anyone and would return to Alaska to work in his family's shrimp business. Barbara Mackle, who by then had married her college fiancé, did not oppose the parole either. It was a done deal, and Krist walked out of prison in 1979—even after being implicated in a prison chapel fire.

Once out of prison, Krist wanted to begin taking classes to become a doctor, his alleged lifelong dream. No reputable medical school would have him, however, and it wasn't until Morris pressured the governor for a pardon that Krist was able to attend medical school in the Caribbean. He graduated in the mid-1990s but could not find work in the United States. Instead, he worked as a doctor in Haiti until he was finally able to land a job in rural Indiana. There, he practiced medicine until a local newspaper dug up his past and he was forced to resign. His medical license in Indiana was also revoked.

This started his descent back into a life of crime. In the fall of 2001, Krist and his stepson, Henry Jackson Greeson, founded Greeson & Krist Construction, which specialized in sheet metal fabrication and bulletproof rooms. Although there was money to be made in construction, much more could be made in drug trafficking, and with Krist, it was always all about the cash. In 2004, he and Greeson began importing cocaine from Cartagena, Colombia. The charter company they used to make the drug runs became suspicious, however, when maps of the Colombian coast were found onboard after the boats had been returned. The charter company went to the authorities, who placed a tracking device on the next vessel Krist rented.

When Krist returned to Mobile Bay, Alabama, in March 2006, he was met by local, state, and federal authorities who had many questions for him. Onboard, they found four illegal aliens who had paid Krist $6,000 each for transport to the United States, along with more than thirty-eight pounds of cocaine in paste form. It was believed that Krist bought increasingly larger amounts of cocaine on each trip with the profits from his previous sales. Once again, it was his greed that did him in.

Based on the international drug-trafficking charges Krist was facing, authorities easily obtained a search warrant for his home, about thirty-five miles east of Atlanta. They found an underground lab where Krist and Greeson were able to convert the paste to the more lucrative powder form of cocaine, which was then sold in nearby Atlanta. The lab also featured a twenty-yard escape tunnel that ended in a fifty-gallon rain barrel. In 2007, Krist pleaded guilty to drug smuggling and was sentenced to less than six years in prison.

Turns out the "Einstein of crime" was not very bright and ended up right back where he started . . . behind bars.

CHAPTER 5

1974: Ted Bundy's Reign of Terror

Ted Bundy, with his all-American good looks and practiced hapless demeanor, was not someone to be feared . . . or so his victims thought until it was too late. He had no problem gaining their confidence with his charm and wit. He often lured his victims into his car and to their deaths. With a clever use of props—crutches, slings, and even fake plaster casts—Bundy was able to earn the trust of the people he would ultimately harm.

By the time he made his way to Florida in 1978, he had all but perfected his technique and had likely killed more than thirty young women before he ever walked through the front doors of the Chi Omega sorority at Florida State University in Tallahassee. But the crimes perpetrated that night at the sorority house were the murders for which he was ultimately put to death.

Years before his Florida killing spree, Bundy's first victim was Joni Lenz, an eighteen-year-old University of Washington student. The twenty-seven-year-old Bundy entered her basement bedroom just after midnight on January 4, 1974. While she slept, he bludgeoned her with a metal rod he had taken from her own bed. He then sexually assaulted her before making his escape. Her roommates found her the next morning in a pool of blood. She had suffered permanent brain damage and was in a coma for ten days, but she survived the attack.

A little less than a month later, Bundy attacked again. His next victim was his cousin's roommate and another UW student, Lynda Ann Healy. Bundy entered her room, knocked her unconscious, and dressed her in some clothing from her closet before carrying her sheet-wrapped body off with him. Her roommates said they heard nothing until the next morning, when her alarm was going off incessantly. Healy had a job at a local radio station doing ski reports and was usually up and out of the house just after 5:30 A.M. When her roommate went into her room on the morning of February 2, 1974, to turn off the alarm, she noticed Healy's bed was made and just assumed the young woman was already on her way to work. She could not have been more wrong.

While she was in the room turning off the alarm, the bedside phone rang. It was someone from the radio station, asking if everything was okay with Lynda. The roommate assured the folks at the radio station that Lynda was on her way and would likely soon arrive for her shift. It was not until her parents called in the early evening hours to learn why Healy had not arrived for a prearranged dinner that the first tremors of alarm were felt. No one had seen Lynda for almost twenty-four hours, so her parents called the police. They came to the apartment to investigate and spoke with her roommates. It was then that they discovered some startling facts that might otherwise have been overlooked. Although one roommate had seen the neatly made bed and assumed that Healy had arisen early, made her bed, and then left for work, another told police that Lynda was not in the habit of making the bed at all. When the police searched the room, they determined that the top sheet and one pillowcase were missing. They also found bloodstains on the pillow and bottom sheet, which later were determined to be the same blood type as Healy's. There was also blood on her nightgown found hanging in the closet. Some of her clothing was missing, and one of the doors to the house was unlocked. Panic began to set in. Lynda Healy's body would not be found until the first week of March 1975.

Bundy now seemed to have acquired a taste for killing, and his spree began to escalate. His next victim was Donna Gail Manson, a nineteen-year-old student at Evergreen State College in Olympia, Washington, who disappeared from the campus on March 12, 1974. She had been on her way to a school concert when she had a fatal encounter with Bundy.

Susan Elaine Rancourt, a student at Central Washington State University (now Central Washington University) in Ellensburg, was Bundy's next victim. The eighteen-year-old disappeared on April 17, 1974. A few nights later, two students at the university told authorities that a young man with his arm in a sling had asked for their help in carrying some books to a Volkswagen Beetle that night.

Bundy's next victim was Roberta Kathleen Parks, a twenty-two-year-old student at Oregon State University, who disappeared on May 6, 1974.

Brenda Carol Ball was Bundy's next victim, and his first deviation from his usual type—Ball was not a college student. She was last seen with friends in the Flame Tavern in Burien, Washington, on June 1, 1974. After she left alone, she was not seen alive again.

Georgann Hawkins was an eighteen-year-old freshman at the University of Washington. She disappeared on June 11, 1974, from an alleyway behind her on-campus sorority house, Kappa Alpha Theta. She was walking home from her boyfriend's residence hall room when she was abducted by Bundy. A young man with a leg cast had been seen by several other students, and they said he was trying to manage a briefcase along with his crutches. He would have made quite the picture of helplessness that night. The students told authorities he approached them and asked for help in getting the briefcase safely to his car, a Volkswagen Beetle.

His next victims marked the first time Bundy kidnapped two women in the same day. The incidents were separate, however. Janice Ott, age twenty-three, and Denise Naslund, nineteen, both disappeared from a state park on July 14, 1974. The two young women disappeared after each was seen talking to a young man who was struggling with a sailboat and what appeared to be a broken arm. Eight separate witness accounts detailed that a young man named "Ted" had been seen in the area. Five of the eyewitnesses were women who told police that Ted had asked them for help loading his sailboat into his car. Three more witnesses later said they had seen Ted approach Ott with the boat story and saw her, unfortunately, walk away with him. Naslund disappeared just a few hours after Ott. Their remains were found by hunters on September 7, 1974, just about a mile from the park. Police were baffled by an extra femur bone that was found in addition to the women's remains. Bundy later said that the leg bone belonged to Georgann Hawkins.

Carol Valenzuela, age twenty, disappeared near Vancouver, Washington, on August 2, 1974, the last of Bundy's victims in this state. But Bundy had left police with a few important clues before leaving Washington: his first name, a physical description, and the make of his automobile.

Deciding a change was in order, Bundy moved to Utah to attend law school. With his eye firmly set on a career in politics, he believed becoming a lawyer was tantamount to his success. The change of scenery fit in nicely with his plans. It was, however, not very nice for several young women who would come to meet Bundy during the course of the next few months.

Nancy Wilcox, sixteen, disappeared from Holladay, Utah, on October 2, 1974. Just before he was executed, Bundy confessed to Wilcox's murder and detailed it for investigators. He said that when he abducted her, he intended only to rape her, because he was trying to "de-escalate" his behavior. However, he strangled her to death when he was trying to silence her screams.

The last person anyone would expect to be kidnapped at the hands of Ted Bundy would be the daughter of a local police chief. But Bundy likely had no idea what Melissa Smith's dad did for a living, and anyway, he did not play by the rules. The seventeen-year-old disappeared from Midvale, Utah, on October 18, 1974. A postmortem examination showed that she had been alive for about five days, during which time Bundy raped and sodomized her, before finally strangling her.

Laura Aime, a seventeen-year-old, disappeared on October 31, 1974, after leaving a Halloween party in Lehi, Utah. Hikers found her naked, beaten, and strangled corpse on Thanksgiving Day.

Carol DaRonch, eighteen, was the lucky one—she was the only one of Bundy's victims able to escape from his car. Usually, once a victim was in the car, she was his for the taking. DaRonch, however, was different. The killer tried to kidnap her in Salt Lake City on November 8, 1974, but she escaped and was able to later give testimony at his trial. Bundy claimed to be Officer Roseland with the Murray Police Department and approached DaRonch as she left a local mall, telling her something had happened to the car she had left in the parking lot. Bundy told her he thought she ought to come with him to the police station. She agreed to the request but refused to put on her seat belt once in the Volkswagen Beetle—marking one of the only times failure to buckle up actually saved a life. When Bundy abruptly pulled to the side of the road, she was able to maneuver away from him when he tried to handcuff her. In their subsequent struggle, Bundy latched both cuffs to the same wrist. When he tried to strike her with a crowbar, she was able to catch it moments before it slammed into her skull, and then broke free and jumped out of the car.

DaRonch's frustrated would-be killer was not satisfied, so he went after seventeen-year-old Debby Kent, albeit by coincidence and not a premeditated plan. At this point, Bundy was likely rabid with need and not thinking clearly. He usually operated in a much different manner and away from crowds. This night, however, he had been frustrated by his first victim escaping and was acting in a somewhat scattered manner. Gone was the mild-mannered and fumbling killer. In his place was a young man who unwittingly called a great deal of attention to himself at a play at the nearby Viewmont High School in Bountiful, Utah.

Bundy showed up in the school theater about an hour after DaRonch's escape. A play was being performed by the drama club, and plenty of people were milling about both backstage and in the audience. Bundy did not blend into the crowd as he usually did, and several people noticed him hanging around the back of the theater during the performance. The drama teacher and a student later reported to police that a man who fit Bundy's description asked each of them to come with him to the parking lot to help identify an automobile. As they lived to tell their tale, both obviously refused to help Bundy with his quest. The drama teacher told authorities she saw Bundy about an hour later, with his shirt untucked, breathing heavily, and his hair a mess . . . and what could he have been doing to be in that condition when just an hour earlier he looked like any other clean-cut college student? Another student remembered seeing a man hanging around the back of the theater. One student did not live to tell her tale of an encounter with Bundy, however: Debby Kent left the play at intermission to pick up her brother and was never seen again.

Bundy made a few vital mistakes that night. After letting DaRonch get away, he accidentally dropped the key to his handcuffs in the parking lot of Viewmont High School. When DaRonch was questioned by police after her ordeal that evening, she was still wearing the handcuffs her would-be killer had attached to one wrist. After they were called to Viewmont High School to investigate Kent's disappearance and the reports of a strange man lurking about, the police came across the key in the parking lot. Knowing that the likelihood of two such strange occurrences were unrelated was slim, they tried the key in the handcuffs on the shaken woman's wrist. DaRonch was immediately freed, and police had their first solid evidence connecting these two crimes and possibly others.

Caryn Campbell, a twenty-three-year-old nurse, disappeared from her Snowmass, Colorado, hotel on January 12, 1975. She had been vacationing with her fiancé and his children when she vanished from the fifty-foot span of carpeted hallway between the elevator doors and her hotel room. Her body was found just outside of Snowmass on February 17.

Julie Cunningham, a twenty-six-year-old ski instructor who also worked in a local sporting-goods store, vanished from Vail, Colorado, on March 15, 1975. Bundy later told investigators that he had approached Cunningham on crutches and asked for her help in carrying his ski boots to his car. Once there, he grabbed a crowbar he had placed under the car and hit her over the head, handcuffed her, and then strangled her.

Denise Oliverson, twenty-five, disappeared from Grand Junction, Colorado, on April 6, 1975. The homemaker's bike was found abandoned under an overpass. Her body was one of the few never recovered.

Lynette Culver disappeared on May 6, 1975. Bundy snatched the twelve-year-old from her junior high school in Pocatello, Utah, and took her to his hotel room, where he raped and then drowned her. Although he usually liked his victims a bit older, with long hair parted straight down the middle, tall, and slim, he occasionally deviated from his modus operandi and snatched a much younger girl. Culver was one of the unlucky ones.

Just a week later, Melanie Cooley, eighteen, vanished from Nederland, Colorado.

Shelly Robertson, twenty-four, was abducted from Golden, Colorado, on July 1, 1975. Later that month, Nancy Baird, twenty-three, disappeared from the Layton, Utah, gas station where she was employed. These were the last of the Utah killings. Bundy would soon spread his terror to a much milder clime—Florida.

Margaret Bowman, twenty-one, and Lisa Levy, twenty, Chi Omega sorority sisters at the University of Florida, were bludgeoned and strangled to death on January 14, 1978. Karen Chandler, twenty-one, Kathy Kleiner, twenty, and Cheryl Thomas, twenty-one, were also viciously attacked that night, but all three survived.

His last victim was another twelve-year-old, Kimberly Diana Leach, who vanished from her junior high school in Lake City, Florida, on February 9, 1978. She was another departure from his norm, but it is believed that at the time, Bundy was just attacking to attack. He was no longer following any set pattern, because his need had become so great.

Bundy was no stranger to crime even before he became one of the most active serial killers in history, at least in this country. His first arrest was on August 16, 1975, when he failed to stop for a police officer. The officer became suspicious when Bundy turned off his car lights and began running stop signs. A search of his car revealed a ski mask, another mask made from women's pantyhose, a crowbar, handcuffs, trash bags, rope, an ice pick, and other burglary tools. Curiously, the front passenger seat of his car was also missing. Bundy was seemingly unfazed during the police interrogation and had ready explanations for the items that had been found in his Volkswagen Beetle. But the police were unmoved and arrested Bundy on suspicion of burglary—for the moment.

One person not buying his story was Utah detective Jerry Thompson, who will forever be known as the man who was able to connect Bundy and his Beetle to DaRonch and some of the other missing young women. Thompson knew that DaRonch had described some of the same items found in Bundy's VW as those in her attacker's. When the arrest was made and items in the car detailed in a police report, Thompson put two and two together and came up with Bundy. With probable cause, he was able to obtain a search warrant for Bundy's apartment. There he found several more items that linked Bundy to some of the murders and missing persons cases that were under investigation, including a guide to Colorado ski resorts with a check mark next to Snowmass and a brochure advertising the play from which Debby Kent had disappeared.

When the police brought Bundy in for a lineup for DaRonch and some of the Bountiful-area witnesses, all were able to identify him immediately as either "Officer Roseland" or the man they had seen in the back of the theater the evening of the play. It looked as though the police had their man. Bundy was charged with attempted kidnapping.

Bundy went on trial and was convicted of kidnapping DaRonch. He was sentenced to fifteen years in the Utah State Prison. While Bundy had been on trial for kidnapping, Colorado investigators were investigating his possible involvement in the murders in their state. When his credit card activity placed him in the area of several of the murders, authorities believed that once again, they had their man. Colorado pursued murder charges in the Caryn Campbell case, and Bundy was extradited to the Centennial State to stand trial.

Bundy's Colorado trial took place in the two-story Pitkin County Courthouse in Aspen. During a recess in the trial in early June 1977, Bundy, who was acting as his own attorney, was allowed to go to the courthouse's law library to do research. There he jumped from the second-floor window and escaped. He managed to avoid custody for six days, but then was caught by two police deputies who noticed a Cadillac with dimmed headlights driving erratically. After they pulled the vehicle over and approached the driver, they recognized Bundy and took him back to jail.

Bundy escaped again on December 30, 1977, after acquiring a hacksaw and starving himself. He sawed through the welds in a small metal plate in the ceiling of his cell, and then squeezed up and into the crawlspace. He had lost enough weight from the extreme dieting to be able to fit through the tight hole and maneuver through the confined space in the ceiling. From there, he made it into the jailer's apartment and walked right out the front door.

At 3 A.M. on January 15, 1978, Bundy walked into the Chi Omega sorority house at Florida State University in Tallahassee and killed two sleeping women before attacking two more of their sorority sisters. He then broke into another home and viciously attacked another FSU student, severely injuring her.

A month later, and after killing one more young girl, Bundy was apprehended for good when an alert Pensacola police officer stopped him just a little after 1 A.M. and ran a check of his license plate. When it came back as stolen, the two scuffled, and Bundy was eventually arrested. The next day, he was positively identified through fingerprints and was charged with the Chi Omega murders.

He stood trial in Miami after a change of venue from Tallahassee. Bundy once again acted as his own attorney during the proceedings. Nita Neary, another member of Chi Omega, identified Bundy in court as the man she saw leaving the house in the early morning hours after her sorority sisters were attacked and killed. Forensics experts were able to match a bite mark on Lisa Levy's buttock to a mold of Ted Bundy's teeth. Bundy was convicted on all counts and subsequently sentenced to death by electric chair. He was also tried in Orlando for Kimberly Leach's murder—though he did not act as his own attorney this time—and was found guilty on all counts and again sentenced to death.

Bundy's life began in a home for unwed mothers in 1946. His grandparents, trying to save the family's reputation, claimed him as their own. Though accounts vary, it is widely believed that Bundy thought his mother was his sister until he graduated from high school. Bundy's own story changed throughout his life, and no one is really sure what he knew when, but it is believed that the events of his early life may have been at the root of his later apparent need to kill. He never knew who his father was, and his mother gave conflicting reports throughout her life as to his identity. When Ted was five years old, his mother took him and moved to Tacoma, Washington, where she married Johnnie Bundy, who legally adopted Ted and gave him his surname.

Bundy had a self-described awkward childhood and teenage years. He said later in life that he never really felt that he fit in and was not really sure how people went about making or keeping friends. It was a skill that always eluded the naturally shy teen. Bundy's shyness kept him out of the dating realm well into his college years. He originally attended the University of Puget Sound but soon transferred to the University of Washington.

His love life never really took off the way he wanted it to. He fell in love with a co-ed at the University of Washington who was in every way out of his league—financially, socially, and academically. She ended their relationship after deciding that Bundy was not husband material. He sank into depression and quit school for a time. After Bundy graduated from college and entered law school, the young woman who had broken Bundy's heart reentered his life and was instantly enamored with the now confident young law student. Bundy proposed and she accepted. He ended the relationship just two days later, however, refusing to return her calls or see her in person. He later told investigators that he did this because he just wanted to prove to himself that he could have her if he wanted her. It was just after the breakup that the killing spree began.

Throughout his life and beginning in his early childhood, Bundy was a habitual liar and compulsive thief. He was arrested twice as a juvenile, but his record was expunged. He continued lying and stealing throughout his life, and both traits played into his future as one of the most prolific serial killers of all time.

Bundy majored in psychology in college and, ironically, volunteered in a suicide prevention center alongside the now famous crime writer Ann Rule. It was she who first clued police in to the possibility that her friend Ted Bundy might be responsible for the many deaths of young women in Washington, Utah, and Colorado. She was researching his crimes when she made the connection between the young man she had volunteered beside and the terrifying killer. He had so perfected the genial-psychology-major-turned-law-student act that even a trained journalist did not see through the persona he had created to discover the killer within. But Bundy, a confident, affable, intelligent young law student, was the last person police would have suspected of the gruesome attacks and murders. Rule eventually wrote a book about Bundy called *The Stranger Beside Me*.

Bundy lived out his days on death row in Starke Prison in Starke, Florida, and exhausted all appeals of his case. He met with several investigators and criminal behaviorists while he waited for death and gave them many details of his crimes. His words and actions gave them great insight into the way his mind worked, or didn't, as the case may be. He also confessed to several previously unsolved crimes—blaming them on the pornography he saw as a young adult—and no doubt helped many families gain closure. Although the number varies and no one is really sure how many lives Bundy took, estimates range from thirty to more than one hundred. It is likely not even Bundy knew the real number. But he finally lost his life at 7:13 A.M. on January 24, 1989, when he was executed in the electric chair. The crowds outside the prison cheered loudly.

CHAPTER 6

1978: The Cop Killer

The canal is not particularly distinctive or memorable. It is a shallow scar running directly east–west in the Boca del Mar section of Boca Raton, a place once covered by acre upon acre of green beans. Today the canal separates a pair of middle-class subdivisions. Aside its south bank sits Amberwoods, a neighborhood that endured plenty of anguish in 2003, when Mark Drewes, a fun-loving youth playing pranks on the night of his sixteenth birthday, rang the doorbell of a neighbor's house in a game of "ding-dong ditch." The neighbor said he thought Drewes was a burglar and fatally shot him.

But Amberwoods was a crime scene well before Mark Drewes was born. On April 21, 1978, laborers were clearing fill from the canal running along the north boundary of Amberwoods when they came across a gruesome sight: a human skull, riddled with bullet holes.

Forensic scientists set to work immediately and within a month identified the skull as that of Leigh Hainline Bonadies, a tennis-loving newlywed who had worked as a waitress. She had left a note for her husband on the door of their home in southwestern Fort Lauderdale. She was going for a little vacation, it said. She'd be back soon. The note was written in September 1969. Leigh was never seen alive again.

Gerard John Schaefer Jr. was born in Wisconsin, spent his early youth in the Atlanta area, and came to Fort Lauderdale with his family in his early teens. Known as "Jerry," he was the oldest of Gerard and Doris Schaefer's three children, with a brother, Gary, and a sister, Sara. Jerry had attended Catholic school in Atlanta and continued doing so in Fort Lauderdale, graduating from St. Thomas Aquinas High School in 1964. He considered the priesthood after high school and applied at St. John Vianney College Seminary in Miami, but he was not accepted. He attended Broward Community College for a while, and then went on to Florida Atlantic University. He attended FAU from 1968 to August 1971, when he received his bachelor's degree.

During his years at FAU, teaching had appealed to Schaefer, and he was twice placed in student teaching assignments at Broward County high schools, Plantation and Stranahan. Both went poorly for him. He then decided on law enforcement as a career. He was hired by the city of Wilton Manors, one of Broward County's smaller communities. He returned to the community college in September 1971 for the police academy and graduated four months later.

Six months later, he had lost his job. Before completing his probationary period, Schaefer had started shopping around for a better-paying position elsewhere, and word had reached Chief Bernard Scott, who at that time was the youngest chief in the state. Schaefer didn't last long on the job. He hung an intoxicated man by his ankles under a bridge, and Scott fired him after learning what he'd done.

But the clock was ticking on Schaefer's law enforcement career even before it officially started. At the police academy, classmates said Schaefer behaved oddly. He had an apparent aversion to washing his clothes, and he was argumentative and continually disruptive in classes. He was no one's idea of a stellar student, and once he was a member of the Wilton Manors police force, his behavior spiraled downward. He was simply an odd duck; he didn't fit in.

Schaefer was married twice. His first marriage was in December 1968 to Martha Fogg, a member of a patriotic singing troupe called Sing-Out 66, with which Schaefer had briefly toured. Fogg filed for divorce in May 1970. Schaefer got married again three months later, this time to secretary Teresa Dean.

After being cut loose from Wilton Manors, Schaefer looked elsewhere for work. His bachelor's degree from FAU made him a plum catch, and he was hired by the Martin County Sheriff's Department in June 1972. But a month later, he was gone from there too. This time the precipitating event was gagging and handcuffing a pair of women hitchhikers to trees on Hutchinson Island, just north of the Martin County line. As he bound and gagged them, he sternly lectured Nancy Trotter and Paula Wells about the dangers of hitchhiking. First Trotter freed herself and escaped, followed by Wells. When he discovered them gone, Schaefer decided to confess his misdeeds to his supervisor, Sheriff Robert Crowder. Crowder fired Schaefer, and then ordered him arrested. The tree limbs the two young women were tied to and the ropes they were tied with remain in the St. Lucie County evidence locker.

Schaefer was convicted of aggravated assault and sentenced to six months behind bars and two years' probation. While he was out on bond before the trial, Schaefer abducted, tortured, and brutally murdered Susan Place, age seventeen, and Georgia Jessup, sixteen, both of Oakland Park, on September 27, 1972. The two young women's dismembered bodies were found at Blind Creek on

Hutchinson Island, a spot the former Martin County deputy knew well.

At the murder trial for Place and Jessup, the blue-eyed, baby-faced Schaefer softened his image with ties, button-down shirts, and pastel cardigans. He denied ever having met Place or Jessup and claimed to have been on an out-of-state hunting trip at the time of the killings. In 1973, he was convicted of their deaths and sentenced to life in prison.

As a boy, Schaefer had liked to torture animals in his Fort Lauderdale neighborhood. And as he grew older, his quarry grew larger. All his victims and suspected victims were female, between age eight and the mid-twenties. In his writings, he suggested that he tired of killing woman singularly and grew fond of "doing doubles." No one will ever know how many women he killed, but the number of suspected victims of Florida's first serial killer hovers around thirty-five.

His youngest victims may have been two Pompano Beach classmates, eight-year-old Wendy Brown Stevenson and nine-year-old Peggy Rahn. Schaefer confessed to their 1969 murders in a letter.

The bodies of some of his supposed victims were recovered, but charges were never filed in those cases, and the bodies of several others were never found. Here are some of the women believed to have been his victims:

- Carmen "Candy" Marie Hallock, twenty-two, a cocktail waitress from northeastern Fort Lauderdale. She had purchased black patent leather pumps and a black cocktail dress for her date with Schaefer, who told her he was a teacher at Broward Community College. She disappeared on December 18, 1969.
- Leigh Hainline Bonadies, who had been married three weeks at the time of her disappearance. She lived in southwestern Fort Lauderdale and had been a childhood friend of Schaefer's, and her brother Gary Hainline had occasionally played tennis with Schaefer.

- Belinda Hutchins, twenty-two, of Fort Lauderdale, who also had dated Schaefer. Like Bonadies, she was married and worked as a waitress. She was mother to a toddler daughter.
- Collette Marie Goodenough and Barbara Ann Wilcox, teenagers from Iowa whose remains were found in 1977 in Martin County.
- Mary Alice Briscolina and Elsie Lina Farmer, both Broward County residents, whose bodies were found buried several hundred yards apart from each other at a construction site in Plantation on January 17, 1973.
- Debora Sue Lowe, thirteen, was a student at Rickards Middle School when she disappeared. She was last seen walking to school on February 29, 1972, and was never seen again.

On April 7, 1973, a few days after the headless bodies of Place and Jessup had been discovered, police knocked on the door of Doris Schaefer's Riverland Road home in southwest Fort Lauderdale. They presented Mrs. Schaefer with a search warrant and went into Jerry's bedroom, which he had told his mother was off-limits to her and everyone else as well. Inside a locker steamer trunk was Schaefer's box of "trophies." The macabre collection contained teeth and bones, weapons, gruesome photographs, costume jewelry, and personal effects from the missing women, including personal papers belonging to Goodenough and Wilcox, Hutchins's address book, and two of Hallock's gold teeth and a piece of jewelry belonging to her. There also were pages and pages of Jerry's handwritten manuscripts—depraved, macabre tales.

The murders of Place and Jessup were the only ones for which Schaefer ever went to trial. He was represented by a public defender, Elton Schwarz. After Schaefer's conviction, Teresa Schaefer divorced her husband and married Schwarz.

In prison, those who spent time around Schaefer said he believed himself to be among the upper strata of inmates. He was described as cocky, imperious, and a snitch. Schaefer spent much of his considerable free time in the prison library filing motions and lawsuits; consorting with murderers such as Ted Bundy, Ottis Toole, and Danny Rolling; and grinding out more of his stories of sex, torture, and violence. Sondra London, another girlfriend from his childhood days in Fort Lauderdale, served as Schaefer's coauthor and published them as *Killer Fiction* in 1997. London went on to become engaged to Rolling, earning Schaefer's enmity.

Gerard John Schaefer, convicted in the death of two women and suspected in the deaths of dozens more, died on December 3, 1995, at age forty-nine after being shanked in a dispute over who got the last cup of hot water from the dispensary at the Florida State Prison cafeteria. Schaefer was stabbed and slashed more than forty times in the face, head, and neck. Vincent Faustino Rivera, thirty-two, already serving life in prison for first- and second-degree murder convictions and a robbery conviction from Hillsborough County, was convicted of Schaefer's slaying.

In 2007, Lake County law enforcement officials said they had closed the books on the deaths of Nancy Leichner, twenty-one, of Largo, and Pamela Ann Nater, twenty, of Clearwater, concluding that Schaefer was the killer. In early October 1966, hundreds of volunteers had helped search the Ocala National Forest, looking for the women. They had come to the forest with their boyfriends, and when the boys went scuba diving at Alexander Springs, the girls went on a hike and were never seen or heard from again. Schaefer had described to Charles Sizelove, imprisoned with him at Avon Park Correctional Facility, how he had abducted and killed the two young women.

CHAPTER 7

1981: The Murder of Adam Walsh

A stone's throw from Interstate 95 in Hollywood is the Hollywood Plaza, a huge marketplace anchored by a Target department store, a Publix supermarket, and a CVS pharmacy, along with restaurants and take-out joints, chiropractic offices, specialty stores, a rehabilitation and fitness center, and an insurance company's headquarters.

In 1981, the center was known as Hollywood Mall, and it was a far different place: a relaxing, airy mall with a sculpture garden, reflecting pools studded with tiny fountains, and lush green plants growing down one side of its main aisle. Intersecting it at the middle was the anchor tenant—Sears.

The Sears store is gone now, another sign of the population's westward migration to Broward County's suburbs. The Sears store at Hollywood Mall, just across the street from the Hollywood Police Department, was well known for another reason too: It was the place where Adam Walsh was abducted, steps away from where his mother shopped.

Adam was a typical six-year-old American boy of the early 1980s, who loved baseball and *Star Wars*. He lived with his parents, John and Revé, in a three-bedroom home in Hollywood, a city that had maintained a small-town feel. Perhaps it was that homey, small-town atmosphere and the inherent trust that comes with it that allowed the Walshes' lives to be altered forever. In 1981, stranger danger was not yet a concept taught to children in preschool. It was still okay for an adult to say hello to a child while out and about. It was still okay for a child to be separated by a few steps from a parent or other caregiver. Unfortunately, that would forever be changed by Adam's trip to the Sears store.

July 27, 1981, dawned hot and muggy, but things still needed to get done. That fateful morning, John Walsh left as usual for the office, Revé planned her day over a cup of tea, and Adam watched morning cartoons. Revé was ultimately headed to the gym, and while she was there, Adam would stay with John's mother, affectionately known as Gram. But first Revé needed to run a few errands, so she made Adam lunch and then asked him to put on the outfit she had chosen for him—a red-and-white-striped short-sleeved polo, green running shorts, and a pair of tennis shoes. Adam, being six, decided against the sneakers and opted instead for yellow flip-flops, the "state shoe" of Florida. He topped it all off with his beloved beige captain's hat.

Mother and son hopped into the car and left to run errands. They stopped at Adam's school, where Revé dropped off a tuition check. Next up was the Sears store. Revé knew brass lamps were on sale, and she wanted to see if they might work well in their home. She parked where she always did, on the north side of the receiving dock. They crossed the parking lot holding hands, just as they always did. They entered the store through the north entrance, just as they always did. They went to the toy department, as usual. What was not usual was a huge new display for a video game, where several children had gathered around, playing the game. Adam asked for permission to stay and watch. She agreed and stepped a few aisles away to look at lamps. It was about 12:15 P.M.

When she returned, Adam was gone. At about 12:22 P.M., she walked up and down several aisles, calling his name loudly. Not only was her son not where she had left him, but all the other children were gone as well. The video game was no longer making its chirps and whirls. Frightened, she located a Sears associate to help her find her missing son. At first the store clerks seemed reluctant to help. They told the worried mother that her son had probably just wandered off or gone looking for her. Revé knew her son, though. She kept insisting that her son never wandered off and something was very, very wrong. The associate finally used the store's intercom system to page Adam and ask him to meet his mother at any one of the service counters in the store. Her anxiety growing by the minute, Revé Walsh searched for her son by herself for two more hours until someone finally called the police. After the police responded and Gram and John arrived to help as well, Revé and Gram searched the store while John worked with the uniformed officers to try to find his son.

Earlier, a seventeen-year-old security guard who had been on the job for only a few weeks responded to a call from the toy department. When interviewed later by the Hollywood Police Department, she said that the four boys there had become loud and unruly, bickering over what was happening on the screen and over the controls for the game. She had approached them and told them fighting was not allowed in the store. She asked the boys, thinking they were together, if their parents were in the store. They answered no. Adam, being the youngest, was probably too intimidated to contradict and tell an adult something different. She separated the two groups of boys and told them to leave by two different exits in the store—two to the north exit and two to the west. If Adam was one of the ones sent to the west exit, he would have been lost, as he always entered and exited the store through the north doors.

Authorities now believe that Adam was outside the store at an unfamiliar exit, waiting for his mother to come find him. It is widely thought that while Adam waited, he was abducted from outside the front of the store after the older boy went on his way. As security cameras were not in use at the time, there is no record of what really happened, only conjecture.

For fifteen days, Adam's mother and father waited for word of what happened to their young son. While they waited and prayed that he would be returned safely to them, friends and family papered the area with flyers that had a picture of a smiling little boy, sans one tooth in front. More than 150,000 flyers were posted in the Hollywood area and beyond. The Walshes hoped the flyers would trigger someone's memory or lead them to the missing child. They waited and waited for a call that would bring them hope.

But unfortunately, the next word they received was tragic. Fishermen found Adam's severed head 120 miles away in a Vero Beach canal on August 10, 1981. The rest of his body was never found—even after his killer confessed. The Broward County medical examiner, Ronald Wright, ruled that the cause of death was asphyxiation and not decapitation. Investigators believed that was done to make his remains unidentifiable or keep his cause of death undetermined. Wright said that the condition of Adam's head led him to believe that the child was more than likely killed the same day he was abducted. The Walshes, understanding that his remains could eventually lead to the capture and conviction of Adam's murderer, chose not to bury the only part of his body recovered. Adam's skull still remains at the Broward County medical examiner's office.

That Thanksgiving, two weeks after what would have been Adam's seventh birthday, Revé learned she was pregnant with daughter Meghan. At the time, she told local newspapers that though they were excited about the imminent birth, there could not be any substitute for the son who had been so brutally murdered.

From this point, the case went very quiet. For two years, investigators continued to chase down leads, but with no tangible outcome. They ruled out people and places but were no closer to making an arrest. But then the murderer came forward.

On October 10, 1983, Ottis Elwood Toole, a convicted serial killer and arsonist, confessed to the six-year-old's murder. Toole was serving a twenty-year sentence for arson at Union Correctional Institution in Raiford, Florida, when he told a Jacksonville detective that he had killed a young boy in south Florida. The detective, who had known Toole for almost twenty years, immediately called the Hollywood Police Department, and the lead investigators on the Adam Walsh case raced to interview him that night.

Toole said that he and his lover and partner, Henry Lee Lucas, had abducted a young boy from a Sears parking lot. Putting as much real estate as possible between them and the scene of the abduction, Toole said they headed north on the turnpike toward Jacksonville in a white 1971 Cadillac. Toole said it was Lucas who cut off the boy's head while Toole held him down.

The detectives became skeptical when Toole told them the boy was between seven and ten years of age and wearing jeans, a blue shirt, and tennis shoes. Adam was not yet even seven years old and was wearing a very distinctive shorts-and-flip-flop combination. Getting the age wrong was one thing, but there was no mistaking the outfit Adam was wearing at the time of his disappearance. And when he was shown a photo of Adam, Toole did not recognize him.

Doing due diligence, the detectives ran down Toole's story despite their skepticism. After much investigation into his whereabouts at the time of the kidnapping and subsequent brutal murder, they learned that Lucas was in jail in Virginia, serving a sentence for car theft. When confronted, Toole admitted he had lied, but then told detectives he actually had acted alone in the abduction of the child.

Toole told the detectives he had seen Adam outside the Sears store, looking a bit lost. He said he lured the boy into his car with promises of toys and candy. When he got Adam into the Cadillac, he locked the doors and windows immediately and drove north to Jacksonville. As Toole described it, Adam was initially very quiet and docile, but then became agitated and insisted they return to the Sears store. Toole continued driving, but Adam began screaming.

Toole pulled off the turnpike at a service plaza and choked the boy to quiet him down—likely killing him at that time. Toole said he was afraid Adam would lead police to him if he let him go, so he kept searching for a place to end Adam's life and any chance that the boy would recognize him later.

Toole eventually found an area that would meet his needs. He pulled off the turnpike and under cover of a wooded area, where he used a machete that he kept under the front seat to chop off Adam's head. Toole told the detectives it took several blows and both hands to sever the boy's head. He buried the body but took the head with him, first placing it on the floorboards of both the front and rear seats—an important fact later in the investigation. He threw the head into a canal and continued on his way north to Jacksonville. Toole told investigators, when asked, that Adam never regained consciousness after he choked him. Many believe Adam was dead long before Toole took the machete to him.

Detectives believed Toole in part because of his demeanor while recounting the story—he was tearful and seemed remorseful. Though he was a habitual confessor to homicides he had not committed, this time Toole was different. They had not seen this type of emotion in him before. In the past, he was boastful when talking about the details of the crimes. But this time, he was very different, and it gave detectives pause. He also got several of the details correct—and they were consistent with the findings of the medical examiner. Unless one was involved in the crime, it is pretty hard to guess at the correct number of blows it takes to sever a head. Toole got it right.

The first thing investigators felt they had to do to determine whether Toole was telling the truth was to find the Cadillac that Toole said he had used to make his getaway. This was accomplished in relatively short order. The car was found on a Jacksonville used-car lot, awaiting its next owner. Luckily for the police, it had not yet been sold and was easily accessible to them. Initial testing showed the presence of blood on the floorboards, right where Toole said he had placed Adam's severed head. The Hollywood Police Department turned the car over to a law enforcement lab in Jacksonville to process the evidence for them. This was standard operating procedure at the time, and no one thought anything of it. Some of carpet was removed for in-depth testing.

Just two short weeks later, on October 21, 1983, Toole was brought back to Hollywood under extremely tight security to walk detectives through his steps the day Adam disappeared. Toole was able to correctly identify the abduction site and the canal where the head was found, but not the area where he claimed to have buried the body. The police, however, were anxious to close the case. They called a press conference that evening and announced that the murderer of Adam Walsh had been located, had confessed, and was behind bars. The children of Broward County were once again safe.

One family would never feel safe again. John Walsh made a statement the next day, saying that he missed Adam more now, but that he hoped justice would be served and his son might finally rest in peace with his alleged murderer behind bars where he belonged.

It would not happen that day. There was no physical evidence to tie Toole to the case, and the police did not get it for another two decades. A search of the area where Toole said he had buried the body turned up nothing. Even Toole began to question his own story, telling police that if he had killed the young boy, he should be able to find the body. But he could not.

Three months later, Toole decided he had had nothing to do with the murder at all and told investigators he had made it all up. And once he recanted, someone in the crime lab deemed the carpet samples irrelevant and threw them away. First sold to a used-car dealer, the car was eventually scrapped. The only physical evidence investigators would ever have was gone forever. The Walshes and the Hollywood police were right back where they had started—a murder without a murderer.

Toole was born in Jacksonville, Florida, in 1947. Abandoned by his father as a young child, he was raised by his mother, a religious fanatic. Toole was sexually abused by his mother and other close relatives and was forced to wear girl's clothing. His grandmother was a Satanist who nicknamed him "Devil's Child."

Reports vary about Toole's intelligence. Some say his IQ was just seventy-five; others say it was much higher but because he suffered from dyslexia and attention deficit hyperactivity disorder, he tested much lower and was often thought to be mildly retarded. In addition to being illiterate and suffering from myriad learning disabilities, Toole was also an epileptic and experienced frequent grand mal seizures.

Toole's life of crime began at a young age. He often ran away from home and set abandoned buildings on fire, which he said he found sexually arousing. And sex seemed to play a central role in Toole's life. From the age of five on, he had several stories of abuse, neglect, and homosexual relationships. He became sexually active at the age of twelve, when he began a relationship with another child in his neighborhood. Toole began visiting gay bars during his adolescence and became a teenage prostitute. He later told investigators he killed for the first time at age fourteen, when he ran over one of his "johns" with the victim's own car. His first arrest came at the age of seventeen.

From that point until 1973, information about Toole is sketchy at best. It is widely believed that during that time, he drifted through and around the southwestern United States, supporting himself by turning tricks and begging. He was also thought to have murdered two young women, though nothing was ever proven and no charges were brought.

He began hitchhiking throughout the South. During his travels, he met and married a woman who left him just three days after their January 14, 1976, wedding when she discovered he was a homosexual. It was the next year that Toole met Henry Lee Lucas. They soon developed a relationship that was sexual in nature and would lead to, Toole asserted, more than one hundred murders. He said the murders were often carried out at the request of "The Hands of Death," a secret cult to which they both belonged. A practicing cannibal, Toole was able to give detailed accounts of most of the gruesome murders. But it still remains unclear as to how many murders the pair actually committed.

As a whole, authorities are divided as to the authenticity of most of Lucas's confessions. Although Lucas was thought to be the most prolific serial killer in America—killing one person about every five days during his peak of activity—authorities charged with validating his claims think evidence points to about half that number, about 350 deaths.

No one doubted the authenticity of Toole's life of crime. In April 1984, he was convicted and sentenced to death for the murder of a sixty-four-year-old man. Toole locked the elderly man in his home, set it on fire, and walked away. Later that same year, Toole was also found guilty of the murder of a nineteen-year-old Tallahassee resident. For that, Toole received a second death sentence. He appealed, and both sentences were commuted to life in prison. He died of liver failure in prison on September 15, 1996, at the age of forty-nine.

His death came as a shock to law enforcement officials, who had been unable to extract a deathbed confession from him. His niece, however, told John Walsh that her uncle told her on his deathbed that he was the killer of Walsh's young son. John Walsh said he never doubted it—even though the police tried many suspects on for size against the facts of the case.

Suspects in the case were a veritable who's who in the world of infamous serial killers. Jeffrey Dahmer, one of the most heinous criminals of all time, who was suspected of killing more a dozen young men and even boys and arrested in 1991, was at one time named as a suspect in this killing. Many have suggested Dahmer may have had something to do with Adam's disappearance and subsequent murder, but the allegations only became widespread in 2007. At the time of the kidnapping, Dahmer was living in Miami Beach. However, Dahmer's typical modus operandi did not fit Adam's abduction and murder. Dahmer preyed on young men and boys, his youngest victim being eight years older than Adam. Although he usually severed his victim's heads, nothing else about the crime fit. John Walsh has since come forward and said he does not believe Dahmer had anything to do with his son's murder. Ted Bundy's name was even floated at one time, though he was known for killing young women only.

Although no evidence had been discovered, Hollywood Police Chief Chad Wagner announced that the Walsh case was closed on December 16, 2008. After an exhaustive external review of the case had been conducted, the Hollywood police felt confident enough to announce that they finally had their man—even though he had been dead for several years.

The chief also apologized to the boy's parents for lapses in the initial investigation. When he took over as police chief in 2007, Wagner reviewed the entire case file and then asked a retired investigator to conduct an external review of the facts and evidence to come to some sort of determination. He said that they had devoted many, many man-hours to the case and seeking leads to other potential perpetrators, rather than focusing on Ottis Toole. But Toole continued to be the only real suspect, and Wagner said they had conclusive proof linking him to the crime—though that proof has never been made public. The Hollywood Police Department and the Walsh family finally had closure after twenty-seven years.

Adam's death, while unbearably tragic, has spawned many positive initiatives. Adam's father, John Walsh, became the host of *America's Most Wanted* and an outspoken advocate for victims of crimes. He has made it his life's mission to speak out loudly for victims and their families, who often have no voice of their own or no place to turn. To date, John and the show have helped capture eleven hundred fugitives and recover more than forty missing children over the course of more than one thousand episodes. He has also been honored by three U.S. presidents for his efforts to protect children.

It is also because of the Walshes' efforts that the faces of missing children are on milk cartons, flyers, and shopping bags. And it is because of them that fingerprinting programs were begun and security was increased in schools and shopping malls. Additionally, their efforts helped create missing-persons bureaus in every large police department.

Adam's death also helped in the establishment of the National Center for Missing and Exploited Children (NCMEC) in 1984. Since its inception, NCMEC has assisted in over 165,000 missing-child cases, resulting in the recovery of more than 151,000 children. Adam Walsh Child Resource Centers were founded at four locations throughout the nation; these later became part of the NCMEC. Department stores across the country have adopted Code Adam, one of the largest child safety programs in the nation, to help lost children in hopes that this sort of tragedy will not befall another family. Code Adam was created by Walmart retail stores and named in honor of Adam Walsh. The program consists of a series of procedures stores can follow when a child is reported missing. Since Code Adam began in 1994, it has become a powerful preventive procedure in more than 36,000 stores across the country. Walmart has teamed with other retailers to implement this successful program in their stores as well.

Legislation also resulted from the death of Adam Walsh and the activism of the Walsh family, with the creation of the Missing Children Act of 1982, the Missing Children's Assistance Act of 1984, and the Adam Walsh Child Protection and Safety Act on July 25, 2006, which President George W. Bush signed it into law two days later. The signing ceremony took place on the South Lawn of the White House, where legislators joined John and Revé Walsh on the bittersweet occasion. The bill organized sex offender classification into tiers based on the severity of the offense and created a national sex offender registry that required each state to post offender data on the Internet. The registry lists the offender's name, address, date of birth, place of employment, and photograph. The act has been controversial, however, and only a handful of states are currently in compliance.

At the press conference closing the case on their son's murder, John and Revé Walsh issued a statement: "We can now move forward knowing positively who killed our beautiful little boy. We, along with our children, Meghan, Callahan and Hayden, pray for the thousands of parents of murdered and still-missing children. We continue to fight for their safety, and to make sure that no child—especially Adam—died in vain."

Although the ache in the hearts of their loved ones will never subside, the brutal, heinous deaths of several Florida children have resulted in stronger legislation restricting and monitoring those who prey on children. Additionally, they helped provide resources and sources of support for the families of missing children.

In 1991, a cunning sexual predator named Mark Dean Schwab contacted the family of Junny Omar Rios-Martinez, an eleven-year-old Cocoa boy with a winning smile and a bubbly personality, whose picture had appeared in Brevard County's daily newspaper for winning a kite-flying contest. Schwab, who had just been released from prison that March on a previous sexual assault charge, posed as a photographer from the paper. He got to know the Rios-Martinez family and earned their trust.

Schwab abducted Junny on April 18, 1991, at the Stradley Ballpark in Cocoa, where Junny pursued his other passion, baseball. Schwab drove him to a motel in Cocoa Beach, where he used a knife to cut the clothes off the sobbing boy, bound him, beat him, raped him, and murdered him by strangulation. Schwab then stuffed the boy's lifeless body in a footlocker, wrapped it with rope, and threw it away in a remote part of nearby Canaveral Groves. He then fled to his hometown, Port Washington, Ohio. His aunt revealed his whereabouts to police.

The locker was found a few days later. A piece of the duct tape binding the boy's body had Schwab's fingerprint on it. The twenty-two-year-old Schwab was returned to Florida, and on May 14, 1991, he was indicted for first-degree murder.

Schwab rolled the dice at his trial, waiving his right to a jury trial. In his defense, he wove an elaborate but clumsy tale about a man named Donald, later Doug, who had a chipped front tooth, soiled tennis shoes, and an unkempt appearance, and patched the holes in his car's seat with duct tape. Donald/Doug, he insisted, had forced him to abduct and have sex with Junny. Then, Schwab insisted, Donald had killed Junny.

On May 22, 1992, after three hours of deliberation and contemplation, Judge Edward Richardson found Schwab guilty. Schwab showed no emotion as the verdict was read, but his nearby mother's shoulders shook with her sobs. On July 1, 1992, Judge Richardson sentenced Schwab to death. The Florida legislature subsequently enacted the Junny Rios-Martinez Act of 1992 to prohibit persons convicted of sexual battery against a minor in Florida from receiving early release or gain time.

As the Rios-Martinez family awaited Schwab's execution, Junny Rios Martinez Park was dedicated in Cocoa on July 3, 1998. Schwab's execution did not occur for almost a decade after the park's dedication. Part of the reason was a statewide moratorium on executions ordered by Governor Jeb Bush after errors made in the execution of Angel Diaz in 2006 caused his death to take thirty-four minutes. In 2007, Schwab came within four hours of execution, only to have it put on hold as the U.S. Supreme Court considered whether an execution scheduled in Kentucky violated the Eighth Amendment's ban on cruel and unusual punishment. After the appeals were resolved, the current governor, Charlie Crist, wasted little time signing Schwab's death warrant on July 18, 2007.

Schwab, prisoner number 111129, died much more quickly and peacefully than Diaz—thirteen minutes after the administration of the lethal injection, given on July 1, 2008. He was thirty-nine years old.

On September 11, 1995, nine-year-old Jimmy Ryce rode the school bus to his bus stop in the Redland, in southern Miami-Dade County's agricultural country. From there, it seemed, he simply dropped off the earth.

It was not until several months later, when the boy's bookbag was discovered at the home of a Cuban refugee named Juan Carlos Chavez, that investigators learned the story. Chavez had abducted the boy at gunpoint and forced Jimmy into his truck, taking the boy to his trailer. Here Chavez raped the boy, and then shot him in the back when he tried to escape. After Jimmy died, Chavez dismembered his body and buried it in several planters near his trailer; the body parts were found three months later.

A Florida law, the Jimmy Ryce Involuntary Civil Commitment for Sexually Violent Predators' Treatment and Care Act, was passed unanimously by the Florida legislature and signed into law by Governor Lawton Chiles in May 1998. The legislation, which has been challenged several times, calls for inmates with sexual offense histories to be reviewed by the Florida Department of Corrections, Department of Children and Family Services, and other legal and social service personnel to determine whether the criminal is likely to offend again. On release from jail or prison, such inmates may be held involuntarily for further mental health treatment.

Jimmy's parents, Don and Claudine Ryce, both attorneys, founded the Jimmy Ryce Center for Victims of Predatory Abduction in 1996. The center, in Miami Beach, provides strategies, activities, and resources to increase public awareness of sexual predators and predatory abductions. Its activities teach children Jim's GEMs—Jimmy Ryce's Great Escape Maneuvers—ways they can respond if confronted by a sexual predator. The center also provides counseling and support to parents whose children have been abducted by sexual predators and raises public awareness about sexual predators and child abductions. The Jimmy Ryce Center even provides trained bloodhounds to law enforcement officials to aid in finding abducted and lost children.

The Ryces worked tirelessly to help educate children and their parents about predatory abduction. To help honor the memory of their gentle, loving son, the city of Homestead named a baseball field in Jimmy's honor. Claudine Ryce died of a heart attack in January 2009, at age sixty-six. She is buried at Woodlawn Park South Cemetery in southern Miami-Dade County, next to her son.

At the federal level, the Jimmy Ryce Law Enforcement Training Center was established in 1996 to provide multilayered training for law enforcement agencies handling missing-children cases.

Another piece of legislation that has had a widespread beneficial effect has been Jessica's Law, named in honor of nine-year-old Jessica Marie Lunsford of Homosassa, who was abducted, sexually abused, and killed by a neighbor, John Evander Couey.

Jessica's father discovered his daughter missing from her bed in the family's trailer when he got up in the wee hours of February 24, 2005. Mark Lunsford was an early riser because of his work as a trucker, and Jessica, a quiet, affectionate "daddy's girl" who loved stuffed animals and clothes shopping, liked to rise early as well. But when Lunsford found his daughter's bed empty, he began to panic. The front door, he noticed, was unlocked. Lunsford immediately called for help, and Citrus County law enforcement officers, police dogs, and even common citizens were pressed into service to look for the third-grader. They searched the woods, pastures, and other spots around Homosassa, a short drive north of Tampa.

Couey, a registered sex offender, was not living where he was officially registered; he was staying with a sister and her friends within sight of the Lunsfords' trailer. When law enforcement authorities arrived for a second, more thorough, visit to Couey's sister's trailer, they found an old bloodstain on Couey's mattress. The blood was Jessica's.

Couey, who was on the run in Georgia at the time, was captured shortly afterward, and Citrus County officials, along with FBI agents, paid him a visit in jail there. In time, during a polygraph test, he broke down and admitted he had snatched Jessica Lunsford, sexually assaulted her, and imprisoned her in his closet. In fact, she had been in the closet the first time law enforcement officials visited the

Couey home, but they hadn't searched it. Once Couey had learned that the authorities were searching for him, he decided to bury the girl. He placed her—still alive—in a plastic garbage bag, tied it shut, and buried it under the back porch of a nearby mobile home. During his confession, Couey told the authorities where to find Jessica's body. When forensic experts recovered her body, they noted that she had attempted to claw her way out of the bag after being buried alive.

Couey's trial was set for Lake County, presided over by Judge Richard Howard, but an impartial jury could not be seated. That necessitated a second change of venue—to Miami-Dade County, several hundred miles south. The trial started on February 17, 2007, and concluded on March 7, when Couey was found guilty on all charges relative to Jessica's kidnapping, sexual assault, and murder. Couey's attorneys urged a life sentence, citing the defendant's intellectual disabilities, as his IQ was only several points above the threshold for mental retardation. On August 11, however, the jury voted ten to two in favor of the death penalty, and Judge Howard sentenced him to death.

Well before Couey went to trial, the Lunsford family and the community pressured lawmakers to get tougher on child predators. Legislators responded by enacting the Jessica Lunsford Act, which was signed by Gov. Jeb Bush on May 2, 2005. The bill provided longer prison terms, electronic monitoring of convicted sex offenders released on probation, and increased use of sex offender databases. Proponents of tougher legislation for sexual offenders attempted to get the Jessica Lunsford Act passed into federal law but failed. Still, more than forty states have followed Florida's lead and passed similar Jessica's Law legislation. The various states have imposed other restrictions, such as limiting how close sexual offenders can live to schools and parks.

The state of Florida did not get the chance to carry out the death penalty against Couey, prisoner number 063425, as he died of natural causes in the Union Correctional Institution's hospital on September 30, 2009, at age fifty-one.

CHAPTER 8

1989: Aileen Wuornos's Murderous Spree

The victims of this serial killer likely did not see their deaths coming. Most were men who were hoping for something a bit more fun, having hired or at least propositioned a prostitute for a few hours of adult recreation. None of them thought it would end in death.

But that is just what happened—all seven victims wound up dead at the hand of Aileen Wuornos, one of the few female serial killers known to authorities. She was not the first and likely won't be the last, but she may be the most infamous. Born into a hardscrabble childhood, raised in a situation fraught with death and deception, Wuornos turned to crime and violence. With no chance at a fairy-tale life, she instead lived a nightmare that she shared with at least seven victims along the way.

Her first victim was Richard Mallory, age fifty-one, a five-time divorced electrician from Clearwater. Mallory owned a small electrical shop, and his employees were the last people to see him alive on November 30, 1989—aside from his killer. His car and wallet were found the next day by a sheriff's deputy in Volusia County. Although the body was missing from the scene, personal papers, several used condoms, and a bottle of alcohol were found nearby. His body, still fully dressed, was not found until December 13, 1989. He had hemorrhaged to death from three .22-caliber gunshot wounds in his left lung. His murder remained yet another unsolved case until a John Doe turned up about half a year later.

Using dental records, the police eventually were able to identify the body found on June 1, 1990, as that of David Spears, a Winter Garden construction worker. The forty-three-year-old had left his workplace on May 19 and never arrived at his ex-wife's home in Orlando. Family and friends grew alarmed at his disappearance and called the police. There was no sign of Spears until his pickup truck was found nearly a week later south of Gainesville. When the authorities did find his body—nude, save for a baseball cap—he had been shot six times in the torso with a .22. Even though both victims were shot with the same type of weapon and their bodies had been disposed of in the same manner, police were unable to link the two crimes, and the trail on both went cold.

By the time Spears's body was identified on June 7, things had begun to heat up again. Charles Carskaddon, a forty-three-year-old from Booneville, Missouri, had been missing since the end of May, when he went to visit his fiancée in Tampa. The part-time rodeo worker vanished somewhere along I-75. His naked body was found on June 6. It had been shot nine times with a .22-caliber gun.

The next day, Carskaddon's car was found in Marion County. It was thought that a .45-caliber automatic pistol and various personal items might have been stolen from the car, since they were unaccounted for. It was also the day that missionary Peter Siems was last seen. The sixty-five-year-old former merchant seaman left his home in Jupiter to visit friends and relatives in Arkansas. A missing-persons report was filed two weeks later. Nothing was learned about Siems until his car was found on July 4, 1990, in Orange Springs—

apparently he had never made it out of Florida. His body has never been recovered.

The next victim was a salesman in an Ocala sausage factory. Eugene Burgess was last seen on July 30, 1990, when he left the factory to make his routine sales calls. When he failed to return or otherwise show up back in his life, a missing-persons report was filed the next day. His vehicle was found just two hours later. Law officers found his fully dressed corpse four days later in Marion County. Although it was decomposed, a thorough examination of his body showed he had been shot twice with a .22-caliber weapon. Police found various personal effects near his body, which helped with the identification.

Six weeks later, Charles Humphreys became the next victim. The retired Air Force major and former police chief was working for the state of Florida, investigating child abuse claims in Ocala. When he failed to return home from work on September 11, 1990, his wife became worried and called the authorities. His fully clothed body was found the next day. He had been shot in the head and torso with a .22-caliber pistol. His car was found more than a week later in Suwanee County. Because it had no plate or tags, the car was impounded until the owner could be located through the vehicle identification number. That added several days' lag time before it could be traced back to Humphreys. It was not until mid-October that the connection was made.

Walter Jeno (Gino) Antonio, age sixty, was the seventh—and most likely final—victim of this serial killer. A truck driver from Merritt Island, Antonio was also a reserve police officer for Brevard County. His body was found on November 19, 1990. He had been shot four times in the back and head. His clothes were later found in Taylor County, and his car was found on November 24 in Brevard County. Several of his personal effects were missing—items that would become key in prosecuting his killer.

In only one of the murders had anyone seen anything or was any real forensic evidence left behind. Most of the murders went unwit-nessed, and the locations in which the bodies were found were remote enough that almost no evidence of value was recovered. In the murder of Siems, however, the police had something to go on. Even though the body was never found, someone had seen something and provided details about the two people last seen in the victim's vehicle. Enough details were provided that police artists were able to develop sketches of the two women whom witnesses had seen in the car. One was blond and the other brunette. One of the women had been injured and left a bloody palmprint on the trunk of the vehicle. It was the first break in the case, and investigators were hopeful that the palmprint would become the lead that would take them to the killer or killers.

The police were still unwilling or unable to go public with the fact that a serial killer was stalking the highways and byways of Florida, but the media was ready to plaster it all over the front page and scream it from the top of every newscast, following the adage, "If it bleeds, it leads." A serial killer was stalking the area, and citizens were in danger without even knowing it. Pressure from the media finally worked. Police released the sketches of the suspects on November 30, 1990, and in doing so, unleashed a huge media campaign to find the killer. Tips came flooding in, most of them going nowhere. But by Christmas, police had received several calls that identified the women in the sketches as Tyria Moore and Lee Blahovec.

The real investigative work began then. Police spent hours sorting through mounds of paperwork and following the money trail. Police and journalists know that when you want to get into the thick of things, you follow the money. Detectives eventually traced the women through motel receipts and learned that the woman they knew as Blahovec also used the names Lori Grody and Cammie March Green—aliases she had established earlier in her life of crime. Good police work and fingerprint comparisons connected the rest of the dots. Blahovec/Grody/Green was identified as Aileen Wuornos. Her prints put her in Siems's car in July. They had their killer. Police now started the work of tracking the two women to bring them in for questioning and possible prosecution. It proved not to be too difficult.

One of the biggest helps to detectives methodically tracing Wuornos was that she started hawking the victims' personal effects to raise some much-needed cash. On December 6, she unloaded a camera that had been owned by Richard Mallory. She also sold his radar detector. In Ormond Beach, she sold a box of tools that had belonged to Richard Spears. At that pawn shop, she was forced to leave a thumbprint to complete the transaction. The print matched the one found on Siems's car and those on file in the state of Florida for Wuornos that had been collected following her many arrests. The next day, she sold Walter Antonio's gold ring in Volusia County. Each sale left a trail for the police to follow.

Wuornos was taken into custody on January 9, 1991—more than thirteen months after she began her murder spree. She was arrested on outstanding warrants at a bar in Harbor Oaks. Police were still building the case against her for murder but wanted her in custody as soon as possible. They had a very real fear that if she were left at large, she might kill again. Therefore, an arrest on the outstanding warrants was ideal. It would get her behind bars, keep the citizens safe, and give all the law enforcement agencies chasing her time to finish building their murder case against her.

A big help to the case, the police thought, would be getting to the other woman, Tyria Moore. Moore was not as confident or domineering as Wuornos, and detectives thought they had a real chance at getting her help in completing the case against the killer. They knew she had intimate knowledge of the crimes and therefore would be invaluable to them both now and when the case was ultimately prosecuted. They began searching for her in earnest.

A day later, Moore was found and agreed to help police in return for immunity. She returned with police to Florida and made several phone calls to Wuornos, with the police listening in. Moore begged Wuornos to confess, but she refused, even if it meant sparing her former lover from prosecution. The conversations, though lacking a confession, did help the police ultimately catch Wuornos. In the pair's myriad conversations, they discussed a storage unit Wuornos had rented in her own name—a storage unit containing many personal items that had belonged to the murdered men. The police were able to readily identify the items as having once been owned by the victims. Realizing she had been caught, Wuornos confessed on January 16 to six killings, though she claimed all had been committed in self-defense. She still maintained her innocence in the murder of Peter Siems, whose body has never been recovered.

Apparently not too bothered with her arrest or her involvement in at least seven deaths, Wuornos sold the movie rights to her story soon after her arrest. Surprisingly, three of the top cops who were instrumental in her capture retained attorneys to field offers from entertainment companies as well. They were later embarrassed when their rush for publicity became public knowledge. Wuornos, however, felt no such remorse.

Wuornos's story is a compelling one. She was born to teenage parents who separated before her birth in 1956. Her father, Leo Pittman, was a convicted child molester who hanged himself just after Aileen was born. Her mother, Diane Pratt, was unable to care for Aileen or her brother, Keith, and abandoned them to their grandparents, who adopted them as their own in March 1960.

Aileen's childhood was far from idyllic. At age six, she suffered burns on her face that caused permanent scars and were a source of embarrassment during her teenage years. These probably contributed to her inability to make or keep friends. She was described by many who knew her then as a loner who shied away from crowds and those in her own age group. Her stories of molestation at the hands of her grandfather and having sex with her brother are doubtful. And since both are dead, neither is able to confirm or deny her allegations.

She was having sex with someone, though, and she gave birth to a son in a Detroit-area home for unwed mothers in 1971, when

Aileen was just fourteen. The baby was immediately placed for adoption. Her grandmother, the only mother she had ever known, died on July 7 of that same year. She and her brother became wards of the court soon after, and Aileen began her life as a prostitute.

Her first incarceration came in May 1974, when she was arrested in Jefferson County, Colorado. She was charged with, among other things, discharging a weapon from a moving vehicle. She left town before her court appearance, so an additional charge of failure to appear was also added. In Florida in 1976, Wuornos met Lewis Gratz Fell, a sixty-nine-year-old yacht club president. They married later that year, and their wedding was announced in—of all places—the society pages. The honeymoon did not last long, though, as Wuornos continued to become embroiled in altercations in local bars and was arrested for assault. Fell filed a restraining order against his new bride after she hit him with his own cane. They were divorced nine weeks after the nuptials.

Wuornos was arrested on July 13, 1976, in Antrim County, Michigan, for assault and disturbing the peace after she threw a cue ball at a bartender's head. When the police had her in custody, she was also served with outstanding warrants for previous infractions of the law.

Her brother, Keith, died that month from throat cancer, and Aileen was the sole beneficiary of a $10,000 settlement on his life insurance policy. She blew through the money in about two months and was soon turning tricks again. This time, it was in Florida, a much warmer clime for her trade. The weather might have been nicer, but Aileen was not. She was arrested and sentenced to prison for armed robbery, passing forged checks, and theft of gun and ammunition. She also borrowed an alias from an aunt in Michigan and began going by the name Lori Grody—a name that would come to haunt her later in life as her crimes escalated.

Over the course of the next several months, she was cited for several traffic incidents and arrested for several crimes. Then she met Tyria Moore in a gay bar in Daytona. They became lovers, but their relationship did nothing to stop Wuornos's life of crime. She was soon back in trouble with the law and received several citations for her unruly behavior. Moore played right along with her and soon found herself in trouble as well.

The year 1988 was a busy one for Wuornos. Never one to stay out of trouble for long, she had several run-ins with the law and changed her alias more than once. She, as Cammie March Green, accused a Daytona Beach bus driver of assault when he forced her off a bus. Moore was listed in the police reports as a witness to the alleged assault—a report that was key to establishing a relationship between Moore and Wuornos when authorities began to investigate the two women in the disappearance of Siems. In July, Wuornos's landlord accused her and Moore of vandalizing their apartment, alleging that they tore up carpet and painted walls without permission. Further demonstrating her aggressive nature, Wuornos made threatening phone calls to a Zephyrhills supermarket over a period of six days in November 1988 because of an altercation involving lottery tickets.

She worked bars and truck stops and even resorted to hitchhiking to get a trick and cash. She also turned to theft to supplement her income. In addition to her increased belligerence, Wuornos spent hours talking with Moore about her life and her need for revenge on those she saw as having done her wrong. It was when she acted on this need that her career as a serial killer began.

After the killings were over and Wuornos was behind bars awaiting trial, she replaced Moore with a new confidante. Arlene Pralle, age forty-four, was a rancher's wife and born-again Christian who apparently was nearly as emotionally needy as Wuornos. After starting off as just pen pals, the two eventually began speaking daily by telephone, until Pralle actually legally adopted Wuornos.

Florida's Williams Rule came into play during the Richard Mallory murder trial. This rule allows prosecutors to introduce evidence of prior crimes if it shows a pattern of evil or malicious behavior. Usually, prior crimes are not admissible. But in this case, the defendant's history set up a pattern that was easily and readily identifiable as criminal in nature. Moore, as previously arranged, testified against Wuornos, and her words were particularly damning. Wuornos did not help herself when she took the stand as the only defense witness, with no evidence to support her sometimes outlandish claims. After only ninety minutes of deliberation, the jury found her guilty of first-degree murder. She was sentenced to die.

Over the course of the next several months, Wuornos pleaded no contest to the other murders for which she stood accused. She received a total of six death sentences and recanted most of her accusations of rape.

During her trial, the defense tried to introduce evidence that Richard Mallory was a convicted rapist in Maryland, but it was disallowed. A request for a retrial was denied. However, in late 1992, a reporter helped corroborate Wuornos's claim that Mallory had raped her and she had killed him in self-defense. Michele Gillen, a reporter for NBC's *Dateline*, discovered that Mallory had served ten years for rape simply by typing his name into an FBI database. Until then, prosecutors and Wuornos's defense team had been unable to find any criminal record for Mallory. Wuornos had been telling anyone and everyone that she had not received a fair trial, and it seemed, after this television report, that she had not. Due diligence had not been done. But even Gillen did not call for Wuornos's release. She instead asserted that Wuornos was a sick woman who had killed these men in cold blood, though she took the state of Florida to task for not dotting the i's and crossing the t's after Wuornos confessed.

Although she never admitted to his murder, Wuornos told police she could show them where she had left Siems's body. She was flown at taxpayer expense to Piedmont State Penitentiary near Beaufort, South Carolina, but police were unable to find a body where Wuornos had said it would be. Police believed she had concocted the whole story to get a vacation from prison life. Later, during an interview with a filmmaker—but thinking the cameras were off—Wuornos said the murders were truly in self-defense but that she could not stand being on death row and wanted to die.

After an appeal to the U.S. Supreme Court failed, Wuornos announced in 2001 that she would not seek any more appeals against her death sentence and petitioned the court for permission to fire her attorney. In her petition, she told the court that she had killed the men and would do it again, because she had hate running through her system. She said she was tired of being evaluated and told she was crazy. She said she knew what she was saying was the truth: She would, if released, kill again. The only way to stop her, she said, was to kill her.

Wuornos was put to death by lethal injection on October 9, 2002, becoming one of less than a dozen women in the United States to be executed since 1976 and only the second woman in the history of the state of Florida to be executed.

CHAPTER 9

1990: Danny Rolling and the Gainesville Murders

Gainesville is a small college city in which Saturday football games are one of the major sources of excitement. That's when the blue-and-orange University of Florida faithful come out in full force, celebrating each yardage gain and bemoaning the loss of even an inch. Rabid football fans, both those who attended the university and those who live nearby, look forward to the gridiron season all year long. As soon as one season ends, fans are already turning their attention to the next. Not much can deter them from Gator football and the speculation that always surrounds the upcoming season.

However, one year was markedly different. One year, almost no one was thinking about kickoffs and touchdowns at the beginning of yet another season. One year, all attention was pulled violently away from the football stadium and concentrated instead on the campus itself. One year, the palm trees may have continued to sway and the balmy breezes to blow, but no one took any notice.

That year, 1990, Danny Rolling went on a killing spree during the first week of classes at the University of Florida and took the lives of five young college students, sending the sleepy southern town reeling into a horror from which it is only recently recovering, as landmarks of the killings are finally being torn down, overrun, or just plain forgotten. But for a period of several days at the turn of the last decade of the twentieth century, Rolling had everyone running.

Anyone who has been to college knows what a campus is like in the days preceding the start of the fall semester. Parents are helping move students into residence hall rooms and nearby apartments and houses, and the atmosphere is almost festive as friendships and acquaintances are renewed. It is also a time of great chaos, as no one has yet settled into the routine of the semester, and multiple social events take place across campus and in the surrounding areas. It is a nonstop party, with folks coming and going.

The fall of 1990 was no different. Students were back on campus at UF and ready to begin the semester. The fall traditions were well under way, and the season seemed full of hope and promise. That is, until the first bodies were found. The last weekend of August, Officer Ray Barber of the Gainesville Police Department responded to a call made by the maintenance man of a student apartment complex just off campus. The apartment had recently been rented to two young women, both freshmen at UF. Both girls' parents had been trying to reach them by phone and, growing concerned when they were unable to contact their daughters, they called the apartment complex for assistance. The maintenance man could not open the door to the apartment and summoned the police in the late afternoon on Sunday, August 26.

When Officer Barber arrived, he found the door to the apartment locked and got no answer to his repeated knocks. He tried to use the apartment complex's master key, but to no avail—the door would not budge. He finally broke a glass pane in the door and reached in to manually open it. As it swung open, the door to any normalcy on campus slammed shut. Inside, the officer saw the mutilated corpse of Christina Patricia Powell, a seventeen-year-old from Jacksonville. She was a second-semester freshman, having just completed the summer semester to get a head start on her degree in architecture. A spring graduate of Episcopal High School, she had been the editor of the yearbook and wrote for its literary magazine. She had also been very active in her church youth group. Her murderer had raped her and left her body downstairs.

The body of Powell's roommate, eighteen-year-old freshman Sonja Jane Larson, was found upstairs. A Deerfield Beach native, Larson was studying early childhood education. She had graduated from Ely High School in Pompano Beach the previous year. She was a member of the National Honor Society, Mu Alpha Theta Mathematical Society, Students Against Drunk Driving, and Key Club, and was a manager for the girls' varsity basketball and volleyball teams. She, too, had been raped. Both bodies had been positioned for maximum shock effect in what became a hallmark of Rolling's killing style.

The parents of both young women were notified, and headlines on the front page of nearly every newspaper in Florida screamed the news of the murders in Gainesville. No one yet knew that these would just be the first of many headlines detailing the crimes of Danny Rolling—or that they would not end until his life did.

Christa Hoyt was the next victim to be found. The eighteen-year-old from Archer was a student at Santa Fe Community College in Gainesville. She had graduated in 1989 from Newberry High School, where she was in the band. Now she was studying chemistry at the community college and working part-time as a records clerk for the Alachua County Police Department to put herself through school. She planned to transfer to the University of Florida later in her academic career.

Two of her colleagues at the police station grew concerned when she failed to report for a scheduled shift. One of those colleagues, coincidentally, was the wife of the officer who had found the first two bodies, and she would not be spared the horror her husband had witnessed. At 12:30 A.M. on Monday, August 27, while Gainesville was still reeling from the news of the murdered girls whose bodies had just been found the day before, two officers were dispatched to Hoyt's apartment. When Officers Gail Barber and Keith O'Hara entered the apartment, one of the first things they saw was Hoyt's severed head propped on a bookshelf in her bedroom. She had also been raped.

Rolling was not yet done. His first three killings had occurred in rapid succession. The next two would wait a few days, but the hysteria he left in his wake would not. The campus and surrounding town were all but paralyzed with fear. Just one week after *Money* magazine named Gainesville the thirteenth-safest city in America, it had earned a new nickname: "Grisly Gainesville." It was evident that a serial killer was running amok in the community, and no one felt safe, not even in broad daylight. No one dared venture out alone, and students traveled everywhere in pairs or groups, as did the residents of the city. The school year had just gotten under way, but the campus was all but a ghost town. Most students did not attend class, suspicious of everyone and everything. Everyone was scared to make a wrong move, certain it would end in his or her death. Parents were calling their students all day and night just to hear their voices and be reassured that nothing had happened to their son or daughter. But the fears of two sets of parents were about to be realized, as yet another daughter and a son would soon become Rolling's final victims.

Shortly after sunrise on Tuesday, August 28, police were called to another apartment building near the UF campus. No one was answering the door there either, and the fear was palpable. Tracy Inez Paules and Manuel Ricardo Taboada, both twenty-three years old and UF seniors in their final year of school, were Miami natives sharing an apartment at Gatorwood Apartments.

Paules was planning to attend law school after she received her undergraduate degree in political science. The former homecoming queen had been a member of the National Honor Society at American High School in Hialeah, as well as president of her graduating class. She also played soccer and softball but had not allowed any of her extracurricular activities to interfere with her academics. She had earned top marks, which helped her gain entrance to UF. Taboada had graduated from the same high school as Paules in the same year. There, he was president of the Thespians Club and a member of a service organization, the National Honor Society, and several other clubs. He was also an athlete, playing on the football team. He attended Santa Fe Community College before applying to UF's architecture program, and he was expected to become a member of the UF crew club team. Sadly, Danny Rolling ensured that would never happen.

Instead, Taboada's dead body was found in his bed, and investigators believed he had been attacked while he slept. Paules's body was found in the hallway leading to the bedrooms. The bodies of Taboada and Paules, unlike the others, were not mutilated. Authorities believe this is only because Rolling was scared off during the act and simply did not have time to perform his ritualistic mutilation and elaborate staging of the bodies. Paules was, however, sexually assaulted.

The news spread.

Prior to the discovery of the last two victims, men had felt reasonably safe. All the previous victims had been female. But with the murder of Taboada, the game changed, and young men began to fear that they, too, might become victims of the "Gainesville Ripper," who had been dubbed as such by the local media because of similarities to the Jack the Ripper murders committed more than one hundred years earlier on another continent. No one knew if he or she would be the next victim.

A mass exodus of the campus began. Students had all but abandoned classes after the first three murders; now they began to leave altogether. And as they fled the campus, members of the media descended on the community. The city streets were clogged with fleets of satellite trucks, news cameras, and reporters trying to get the story. Even big-name journalists came to town. Dan Rather, then CBS News anchor, referred to Gainesville as "perhaps the most dangerous place in America." Phil Donahue did his show from live from Gainesville and drew record ratings. It seemed that anyone and everyone who had anything to do with a news outlet was in Gainesville . . . and all the while a serial killer was still on the loose.

People did what came naturally at a time like this: they sought out whatever means of protection or preservation they could obtain. Gun and pepper-spray sales skyrocketed. Locksmiths worked long hours to help assuage the fears of parents living miles and miles away from students who remained on campus or in nearby housing. In 1990, the use of cell phones was almost nonexistent, and parents could not be in constant contact with their students. While their fear was real, they had to rely on more traditional means of communication to assure themselves that their students were okay. Today, as a society, we are much better equipped to deal with this sort of situation. In the years since the murders at the University of Florida, we have dealt with the likes of Columbine and Virginia Tech. Students and parents are in constant contact via cell phones and text messaging. Campuses can get the word out in minutes through email, voicemail, and text messages if a situation occurs that needs immediate attention. Parents can sign up for these alerts as well, and anyone can monitor a school's website for up-to-the-minute information. In 1990, the student population of the University of North Florida was about 36,531. To help and to handle the onslaught of calls from concerned parents, the university set up a phone bank and received thousands of phone calls each day. There was no precedent for a crisis of this magnitude, and parents simply did not know how to respond. So they called. And called. And called.

Up until these three days of terror, there had been deaths like this on campuses, but in those cases, the killer was immediately known. In Gainesville, however, the horror came from the unknown. When would the killer strike again? Where? Who would be next? Could it be that man walking alone late at night? Was it the man in the grocery store? Was it someone just passing through? The questions came fast and furious, and unfortunately, there were no answers to be had. Only more questions and more dread and fear.

John V. Lombardi had just been named as the ninth president of the University of Florida. A lifelong academician, Lombardi came to UF from the prestigious Johns Hopkins University, where he had been provost and vice president for academic affairs. Having been at institutions of higher education for more than twenty-three years as a historian, teacher, administrator, and author, Lombardi was no stranger to campuses, students, and parents and therefore knew he had to be visible and present during the crisis that was plaguing his new campus. He immediately made class attendance optional. He did not and would not cancel classes, but he left it up to the students and their parents to decide what was best for each individual. He also authorized a temporary freeze on tuition and fees. He could not expect folks to pay for classes they were not attending and in the midst of a crisis. He did not want to have these young adults pay fees, add and drop classes, and make other life-altering decisions when no one knew what the next day would bring. His leadership at the time was faultless. He and his administration acted swiftly and in the best interests of the students.

Mark Trowbridge was a hall director for Rawlings Hall on the UF campus during the time of the murders. He applauds Lombardi for making what he called "the best decision of his entire presidency" when he decided to keep the university open. It was an act of normalcy, Trowbridge said, that everyone on and near campus could embrace. It was a signal that life would go on and the students had one another to depend on to get through the dark days. The residence halls were opened to all UF students, and many chose to sleep in the hall lounges, common rooms, or empty rooms, or even triple up with friends. Lights were left on across campus, leaving almost nothing in the shadows.

One person who was definitely not in the shadows was student body president Mike Browne. He was vocal about "his" UF and what the killer could and could not do to him and his fellow Gators.

In a news conference that was carried all over the world, Browne told anyone who was watching that the University of Florida was his university, and he would not permit anyone to take it away. He urged his fellow Gators to return to campus and to class. And they did. They came back despite the rumors of mass graves and more murders and missing persons. They came back despite the satellite trucks rumbling throughout the night and the reporters shoving microphones in their faces. They came back to campus and back to class. The university records show that only five hundred students did not come back at all for the fall semester, but even most of those did come back in the spring, when the rumors turned out to be just that.

Another group that refused to stay in the shadows was the police. In fact, they shone lights in all corners of Gainesville, searching desperately for evidence and clues that would lead them to the murderer. More and more members of law enforcement came to campus and to the Gainesville area. A task force was formed to lead the investigation, and members came from several local and state law enforcement agencies. Patrols of the city and the campus were made on foot and by car. Even the student patrol on the UF campus was stepped up. The Student Nighttime Auxiliary Patrol (SNAP) escorted students as they walked across campus. Dozens of new escorts were trained when the demand proved too great for those already on patrol. The local community college, Santa Fe, followed suit and instituted its own patrol. Two of its students, one current and one former, were counted among Rolling's victims, and it wanted to make sure there were no more.

While precautions were being taken to keep everyone in the Gainesville area safe, Rolling was still on the loose. He had been successful in his brutal murders—at least for a time.

Danny Rolling was born in Shreveport, Louisiana, in 1954 to an allegedly abusive father and meek mother. According to Danny, his father, James, abused him until 1990, when Rolling snapped and tried to kill him during a volatile argument. Danny fired several shots at his father with a handgun. James survived, and his son was wanted for attempted murder. He fled to Florida.

It was here that his life of crime began in earnest. As a teen, Rolling had been incarcerated several times for robberies he had committed in Georgia. He had trouble fitting into society and drifted from job to job and place to place. With the attempted murder of his dad, he was forced to leave Louisiana for good. He arrived in Sarasota on July 22 and stayed for nearly a month at two local motels. It was in Sarasota that he attacked and raped Janet Frake. The thirty-year-old real estate agent lived alone. She made a near-fatal mistake on August 5: she left a window unlocked in her home. The masked Rolling used that window to gain entry and lay in wait for her to return. After tying her up and raping her, Rolling decided not to kill her, because she somehow persuaded him to have a beer with her instead. He ended up telling her about his childhood and the abuse he had suffered. After several hours of listening to him and sharing bogus tales about her childhood, she told him she thought it was time for him to leave. And he did, slipping away quietly, only to resurface two weeks later in Gainesville when he checked into a local hotel.

For a long time, Frake's identity was concealed. She never went public, and the media never really knew who she was. She shunned any type of coverage and spent years getting over the psychological ramifications of the brutal attack. It was not until 1995 that she even learned the identity of her rapist. In 1997, Frake sued Rolling for $1 million, but the case was dismissed because the statute of limitations for civil litigation had expired.

In the immediate aftermath and panic of the Gainesville murders, police originally suspected UF freshman Ed Humphrey. The eighteen-year-old was known throughout Gainesville as having a bad temper and displaying vicious behavior on occasion. He suffered from mental illness and was arrested on August 30 in Brevard County for allegedly battering his grandmother. The police thought they had their man in the Gainesville slayings as well. They took fingernail scrapings, blood samples, and bags of evidence to help prove their case. But they were wrong: the real killer was still at large. Humphrey was eventually exonerated of all charges related to those murders, but he was still convicted on October 10 of battery in the case of his grandmother and was sentenced to twenty-two months in prison.

Although they continued to investigate and run down all leads, police were back to square one. They had no real suspects and no idea the real killer was already in custody. Just ten days after the murders, Rolling was arrested for the armed robbery of a local Winn-Dixie after leading police on a high-speed chase. He was charged with attempted robbery and resisting arrest and was left to languish in an Ocala jail. The Gainesville Ripper, unbeknownst to investigators, had been caught. Police, however, viewed Rolling as only a two-bit thief and went about their investigation of his crime as a matter of routine.

Prior to his arrest, Rolling had been staying in a campsite in Gainesville, now the site of a Home Depot. He used the campsite as a home base and a place where he did drugs and plotted more robberies. When police investigated the campsite in late January 1991, the murder case broke wide open. There they came across a cassette tape that contained Rolling's voiced confession. He also confessed to fellow inmate Bobby Lewis that he was the Gainesville Ripper. From there, police were able to link Rolling to all five slayings with evidence they had obtained from the murder scenes, from his campsite, and through DNA. It took five months, but they finally had their man.

Later that year, in September, Rolling was sentenced to life in prison for the robbery of an Ocala supermarket a year earlier, and Ed Humphrey was released after serving thirteen months behind bars. On November 15, Rolling was indicted on five counts of first-degree murder. Although Rolling admitted the facts of his crimes, he insisted they were committed by his alter ego, Gemini. The defense argued that Rolling's actions were uncontrollable because of the abuse he had suffered as a child, but the prosecution argued the opposite. The contention was that Rolling knew exactly what he was doing when he so savagely murdered the five college students, and that his crimes were all premeditated and carried out in cold blood. It was because of his childhood abuse that he knew hurting another human being was wrong. The jury sided with the prosecution and found him guilty on all five counts. He was sentenced to death on each count of murder. Because of this conviction, he would not face prosecution in the Louisiana case of attempted murder.

Although Rolling originally pleaded guilty to the murders and other crimes, he eventually appealed the verdict several times. Behaviorists trained in profiling criminals—analyzing the motives behind the crimes and the manner in which the offenses were committed—believe that Rolling psychologically needed the attention from both the murders and the appeals. The brutal slayings and posing of the bodies suggested to these trained professionals that he wanted to be known. He wanted to be a Jack the Ripper or a Charles Manson or a Ted Bundy. He wanted the community to live in fear of him. He wanted his name to become synonymous with terror. After his conviction, he used the appeals process to keep the spotlight on himself. The seemingly endless appeals kept the vociferous media at his beck and call. Every time he appealed, they came running. His name was splashed across headlines, and his crimes were relived on television. He became infamous.

When time was running out on his appeals, Rolling had one more trick up his sleeve. Through his alleged spiritual advisor, he confessed to the stabbings of a father, a daughter, and her young nephew as they made dinner together as a family on November 4, 1989, in Shreveport. The Shreveport police, after learning about the grisly college murders, had alerted the Gainesville police to the similarity of the crimes. All had been perpetrated with a knife. All were particularly brutal. All victims were posed for maximum impact. The blood type of the murderer was the same. Authorities were convinced the two were linked. Shreveport police did not pursue extradition because they were convinced prosecutors would have an easier time seeking and winning the death penalty in Florida. They were happy to let Rolling face due process in the Sunshine State.

They were right. Despite a last-minute appeal to the U.S. Supreme Court, early in the evening on October 25, 2006, Rolling was given a fatal cocktail of drugs and pronounced dead at 6:13 P.M. at the Florida State Prison, about thirty miles northeast of Gainesville. Witnesses said that Rolling did not have any last words, nor did he apologize to the families of his victims for his actions. Many of the victims' family members were in the gallery, waiting for something from the man who had savagely wrenched their loved ones from them. Instead, he sang a hymn as the dose was administered.

Rolling has become the stuff of legends. His life has been the subject of several books, television shows, and even a full-length movie. The evidence from the trial was eventually made public and then burned to avoid morbid collectors or eBay sales. Unfortunately, in life and in death, Rolling and his crimes are a popular subject. But some good has come out of the crimes and their aftermath. Campuses all across the country have tightened security as a result. Locally, the University of Florida and Sante Fe Community College—now Sante Fe College—are both much more wary during the transition time between semesters and classes. With more than 60,000 people in the area, and almost no bonds having been formed between students yet, it is easy for security and watchfulness to become lax. It is easy to not pay close attention to surroundings when they are unfamiliar and neighbors do not yet know one another. So the police have stepped into the breach with highly visible patrols and escorts.

UF's nationally accredited police force patrols the campus and nearby community in cars, on motorcycles, on bicycles, and on foot. They can be almost anywhere on campus within a few minutes. In addition to the paid professional police force, the university still supports the Student Nighttime Auxiliary Patrol, which will send a van to transport a student anywhere on campus free of charge. SNAP was instrumental on campus and saw a marked increase in service just after the final bodies were found, and it still serves the community today. Students report feeling safer on campus with the very visible police force and the availability of SNAP anytime they are feeling a bit wary about traversing campus on foot.

The University Police Department also established the Voluntary Inspection Program (VIP) in conjunction with local landlords. VIP was developed to encourage apartment complexes to practice safety standards. It is a partnership between local law enforcement agencies, the university, and the Gainesville Apartment Association. Complexes must undergo voluntary inspections by trained law enforcement officers who use the Community Safety Guidelines. If the complex passes the inspection, it is given a free listing on the University of Florida Police Department website and a certificate to display. All this is done in an effort to keep off-campus housing as safe as possible for University of Florida students.

The impact of the crimes has also been far reaching in terms of how campuses and municipalities respond to a campus crisis of this magnitude. Most colleges and universities now have an emergency or crisis plan in place with specific details on how the campus will respond and who has responsibility for what. When emotions are running high, this plan makes it easier to react to a situation. Having emergency plans in place enables campus administration to be proactive if and when a tragedy occurs. Although they occurred decades apart, crisis communication experts agree that because of the Gainesville murders and the lessons learned, the administration at Virginia Tech was much better equipped when a killer came to call. The school had a plan in place and was able to follow it, even amid all the chaos. A tragedy will always be a tragedy, but if some good can come of it, the victims will not have suffered in vain.

The University of Florida Foundation endowed a scholarship to honor the memory of Rolling's victims and to perpetuate their aspirations. Each year, the university awards the 1990 Student Memorial Scholarship to a deserving student who has a 3.5 GPA or higher, with priority given to seniors. And Gainesville has yet another memorial.

Five trees are planted on the campus of the University of Florida, and five more are planted along the median of Thirty-Fourth Street. The five trees in each set represent the five lives that were taken during the brutal three-day murder spree that gripped the campus and community with abject terror. As they bend and sway in the central Florida breezes, they are living memorials of the five lives extinguished by serial killer Danny Rolling.

CHAPTER 10
1997: The Iguana

From 1960 to 1962, an ABC television program chronicled the good, bad, and ugly sides of life on Miami Beach. The setting for *Surfside 6* was a houseboat, and the show's story line was about a detective agency that operated out of it. Troy Donahue was its star. The show had a catchy theme song that changed a bit each week but always ended with this refrain: "And where is it? In Miami Beach . . . cha cha cha . . . cha."

When Andrew Phillip Cunanan got to Miami Beach, all he wanted to do was blend in and avoid capture for four recent murders he had committed. He had one other murder in mind, too, a really big score, and undoubtedly he never imagined breathing his last breath on what could have passed for the set of *Surfside 6*.

Southeastern Florida also has a number of other unwanted exotic species that simply want to blend in. One is iguanas, which have been living in south Florida since the 1950s. They were probably first introduced into the ecosystem when pet owners turned them loose after they grew too large for their cages. In captivity, they made interesting pets; in the wild, the feral lizards grew large, mean, and predatory.

Cunanan had spent his life as a two-legged iguana. He was the youngest of four children born to Modesto "Pete" and Maryann Cunanan. His father was from the Philippines; his mother had been born in Italy. Cunanan's father worked for the navy when Andrew was young. He grew up in the San Diego area and had a rather care-free existence. To his father and mother alike, the baby of the family was the perfect precocious son. He was witty and charming, intelligent, and good looking, and he served as an acolyte at the local Catholic church. Just past the onset of puberty, however, Cunanan started getting in touch with his dark side. He could still easily play the role of the obedient son, but by then it was all an act. Cunanan had come to realize he was gay. Life in the closet held no appeal for him, so living in the shadows and keeping his sexuality to himself at the Bishop's School in La Jolla, California, was never given a second thought. He played his life big and over the top.

About this time, Cunanan became a master of transforming his appearance, behavior, and demeanor to suit and succeed in the environment of his choosing. He was cunning, clever, and manipulative and would do whatever it took to achieve his objectives, but once Cunanan achieved one goal, he almost always wanted more. His theatrical ways constantly made him the life of the party, and he was daring or foolhardy enough that he'd try almost anything, no matter how horrendous, amusing, kinky, terrifying, or just plain stupid it might be. He used alcohol, crystal meth, marijuana, and other substances to prolong and intensify the feelings he got from acting out, but it was never enough.

By early 1997, the twenty-eight-year-old Cunanan's life had taken some turns for the worse. He had gained weight and was no longer a fresh, young thing; his boyish good looks were gone, and he was starting to show his age. Men no longer found him as vibrant and exciting as they had. His savings were gone and his credit cards were maxed out. He was feeling angry and depressed, and it's likely he suspected he had contracted HIV. He was still a bit young for a midlife crisis, but he decided to move on and settle some old scores. He told his San Diego friends he was going to San Francisco and even threw himself a going-away party. The date was April 24, 1997.

Cunanan arrived in south Florida for the last time on May 10, 1997. By then he was on the FBI's Most Wanted list, sought after by federal law enforcement authorities throughout the nation for the murders of four men, beginning with Jeffrey Trail's April 27 murder in Minneapolis and ending with William Reese's on May 9 in New Jersey. In between them, Cunanan also killed David Madson at East Rush Lake, near Minneapolis, on May 3 and tortured and brutally murdered Lee Miglin in Chicago on May 4. Cunanan had come south because he had still one more murder in mind—one that would put his name on front-page headlines across the nation. That murder would take place on July 15 on a glorious, sunny, chamber-of-commerce morning in Miami Beach.

Life in Miami Beach wasn't as glamorous as Cunanan was used to living it. He was accustomed to staying in luxury accommodations. In Miami Beach, his home was the Normandy Plaza Hotel, a small Art Deco place that cost less than $40 a night and had seen better days. Cunanan, who once ate such delicacies as fugu in Japan and ostrich carpaccio in California, now found himself in line at a submarine sandwich store, where he was spotted by the sandwich maker and took off with his tuna salad sandwich before the police arrived.

Internationally celebrated fashion designer Gianni Versace owned the showplace villa at 1116 Ocean Drive in the heart of Miami Beach. Originally built in 1930 for an American oil magnate, Versace, age fifty, bought it in 1992 for $2.9 million. He also bought a small hotel next door and razed it to build a 6,100-square-foot, two-story addition to the home and a stunning swimming pool. All told, the mansion, Casa Casuarina, was 26,000 square feet of solid luxury. Craftsmen had been flown in from around the world to work on the mansion, and no expense had been spared. From the gold toilet fixtures to the Venetian glass tiles that lined the pool, everything was handmade and perfect.

Versace's friends from Hollywood and the worlds of entertainment and the arts visited there often, and he designed theme rooms for them. The home was his special place for relaxation and entertaining, and early on July 15, 1997, he left his home in sandals, shorts, and sunglasses for a stroll to the nearby News Café for some magazines. At about 8 A.M., Versace slid his key into the lock on the wrought-iron gates to Casa Casuarina and turned when someone called his name. Quickly, Andrew Cunanan stepped closer and pumped two bullets into Versace's head. One hit to the right of his nose; the other entered near his left ear. The damage was horrific, and the designer was probably dead before he hit the coral steps to his home. Versace slumped onto the top three steps. Blood and bits of brain matter gushed from his head. At the moment the body thudded to the coral steps, Andrew Cunanan was poised to ascend to the level of celebrity he had always coveted. When word of Versace's murder hit the news wires, he would become America's most wanted person, and the hunt for him would be broadcast worldwide.

But with Versace lying dead in front of him, Cunanan had to act quickly. He took off running. Initially, some of the witnesses to the shooting attempted to chase Cunanan, but seeing the .40-caliber pistol in his hand, they decided to abandon the chase. Police and rescue personnel were summoned immediately, and the massive manhunt began.

Cunanan was quickly identified as the suspect; pictures of him were broadcast widely, and tips began flowing in. Cunanan sightings were phoned in from dozens of locations throughout Miami-Dade County. He also was reported walking along Las Olas Boulevard in Broward County and eating dinner at restaurants in Boca Raton and West Palm Beach, both in Palm Beach County. In the days afterward, Cunanan sightings were phoned in from all around the world.

The reality of it all was radically different. Although he had moved about somewhat freely in Miami Beach before the shooting, Cunanan hadn't gone far after he murdered Versace. He transformed his appearance yet again, shaving his head and growing a little facial fuzz, and he holed up in a nondescript houseboat on Indian Creek about forty blocks from Casa Casuarina. There he lay low, but he knew police were gradually moving in on him.

On July 23 at about 4 P.M., eight days after taking Versace's life and apparently having been unsuccessful in arranging for a fake passport and a ticket to travel abroad, Cunanan was at a low point. The caretaker who looked after the houseboat stopped by to check on it and pushed open the front door, which was cracked open. A moment later, he heard a shot ring out inside. He called 911, and Miami Beach police and Metro Dade officers responded with a SWAT team. They called for Cunanan to come out, but he did not give himself up. Finally, four hours after the episode had started, as darkness was beginning to descend, they donned gas masks, pumped in canisters of tear gas, and went in after him. All the while, helicopters from local television stations hovered overhead, beaming the image around the world. At first the police officers said they found no one inside, but later, they discovered Cunanan's body in the master bedroom on the second floor, clad only in his underwear, dead from a self-inflicted gunshot to the face. Blood had streamed down his face and neck and pooled on his chest, just under his chin. He had left no suicide note. The crime scene technicians completed their work meticulously; they didn't finish with Cunanan's body until almost daylight the next morning.

From altar boy to party boy, boy toy and gay gigolo to spree killer, Andrew Cunanan lived an odd, frenetic existence in his twenty-seven years, and he died on a houseboat in Miami Beach.

Cha cha cha . . . cha.

CHAPTER 11

1997: The Bully

After Gainesville killer Danny Rolling went to prison to complete the appeals process and await execution, the families of his victims tried to resume their lives, attempting with varying degrees of success to fill in the voids left by the violent demises of their loved ones. The Larson family was among them, but the forces of evil apparently weren't quite finished with them. On June 10, 1997, seven years after Sonja Larson's grisly murder, Carla Thomas Larson, Sonja's sister-in-law, failed to return to work from a lunchtime trip to a supermarket.

For most people, a late return from lunch is no cause for alarm. But for the thirty-year-old Carla, it most definitely was. Sonja's death had had a profound effect on Carla, a bright young engineer and mother living in Orlando. After her sister-in-law's death, she became excessively vigilant, obsessed with security and safety. She bought a Rottweiler. She always kept her home and car doors locked. Her Ford Explorer had air bags, an alarm system, and other safety and security systems. She diligently informed those around her where was going and when she'd be back. She expected them to do the same too.

When she failed to return to work after running out to buy some fruit for lunch, and word of her absence spread, her friends and coworkers had good reason to be concerned. They notified her husband, Jim, who was dumbstruck. Jim Larson immediately called the Orange County Sheriff's Department, which responded quickly. The sheriff's deputies were sympathetic to Larson, who already had endured the loss of his sister and was stunned by his wife's disappearance.

A search soon began, and as the hours mounted, Carla's family and friends grew increasingly anxious. Jim, his and Carla's friends, and coworkers at Centex Rooney, where Carla worked as an engineer on the Coronado Springs Resort at Walt Disney World, joined the police in searching for her. Hopes were high that she'd be found alive, but two days after her disappearance, a body was found in an undeveloped area, an overgrown site dotted with palmetto bushes. The body was identified as that of Carla Thomas Larson. She had been strangled.

Carla Ann Thomas was the whole package—she was beautiful with her long, blond hair, highly intelligent, sincere, and vivacious. She met her future husband in their hometown of Pompano Beach, a laid-back community filled with boat lovers, sportfishermen, beachgoing sun worshippers, and weekend warriors. When they met, Carla was a student at Ely High School in the city's western section, a gem of a school set in the midst of a disadvantaged community. The school was the source of pride for the neighborhood and had a sterling reputation for its magnet programs and athletic teams, particularly football. The Tigers sent many of their players on to colleges and from there on to the NFL. After graduating from Ely High, Carla went on to the University of Florida, aiming for a career in construction engineering, a rigorous program for motivated students—one not often selected by females.

James Larson was six years older than Carla and already had graduated from high school when they met. He worked on the ground crew at the Goodyear blimp base on the west side of the Pompano Beach Air Park. The blimp base, now home to the nonrigid airship Spirit of Innovation, is one of the city's bigger attractions. Jim and Carla had dated long-distance throughout her years at UF, but in her senior year, they became a band of three as Jim's sister Sonja enrolled at Florida with the hopes of becoming a teacher. Carla began to function as a big sister for Sonja, keeping tabs on her and helping smooth her transition into college life.

All seemed to be going well until August 24, 1990, when drifter Danny Rolling followed Sonja and her roommate Christina Powell out of a department store and murdered and mutilated them later that evening. Their grisly murders were the first in his spree of terror that gripped the city of Gainesville and kept it in a panic until Rolling was apprehended in March 1992.

Although they wavered and vacillated on their wedding date because of Sonja's death, Jim and Carla were married four months later, on December 1, 1990. The couple moved to Atlanta, where Carla had been assigned by Centex Rooney. The change of scenery didn't seem to help Jim much. Carla saw her husband consumed by anger over his sister's death and spiraling toward depression. She kept urging him to get professional help to deal with resolving his anger, and he finally agreed.

After Carla's Atlanta assignment ended, the Larsons returned home to Pompano Beach for a while, and Jim's moods continued to improve. Not long afterward, the young family got some happy news for a change: they were expecting.

The Larsons' luck, it seemed, had taken a turn for the better. Centex Rooney gave Carla a choice of two Florida sites for her next assignment: Miami or Orlando. Perhaps envisioning many happy family trips to the theme parks that dot the Orlando area, they chose to move to central Florida. Orlando was safer, they told friends; it was a better place for young families. They settled into a small house painted the color of pistachio ice cream in the neighborhood of College Park, fitting it with strong locks and a security system.

Jim's father died in 1996, but their daughter, Jessica, was born that year. She was healthy and beautiful, and the couple started drawing up plans for an addition to their home. Things were definitely looking up. Then Carla went to the store for lunch and never returned.

The *America's Most Wanted* television show, hosted by John Walsh, whose son Adam was snatched from a department store in Hollywood and later murdered, heard of Carla Larson's disappearance and aired a segment on its June 28 show that resulted in a fair number of clues. One came from a woman in nearby Brevard County, who said that a friend of hers, a woman named Angel Huggins, knew about Carla Larson's missing Ford Explorer and would be willing to talk with law enforcement officers.

Angel Huggins, along with her husband, John, from whom she was separated, and their five children, were in the Orlando area on the day Carla Larson went missing, the woman told them. They had hoped a family outing would help patch things up in the marriage. Their motel was across the street from the supermarket where Carla had gone to pick up lunch items. That morning, the Huggins clan had gone to Gatorland, one of central Florida's classic pre-Disney attractions. After their return, John was feeling frisky and wanted sex. Angel didn't, and John didn't like rejection. Their disagreement turned physical, and John grabbed Angel by the neck and tried to choke her, but she managed to break free and lock herself in a bathroom, where she stayed for several hours. When she emerged, he was gone. He returned several hours later, soaked with sweat and with some facial bruises and marks. He said nothing as he rushed into a bedroom and slammed the door behind him. Angel tried to talk to him through the door, with little luck, except for his suggestion that she return home to Melbourne and take the children with her.

Angry, frightened, and puzzled, Angel Huggins drove home and was shocked when John returned home less than a half hour behind her. Parked outside was a white Ford Explorer John said he'd rented. John invited her and the children for a trip to Sea World. She agreed, and the next day, the group headed back to Orlando to visit Sea World and other area attractions.

In the wee hours of June 26, a vehicle resembling Carla's Ford Explorer went up in flames in a secluded spot in Cocoa Beach. It burned fast and hot, and the light and heat it generated drew local authorities to the spot. Very little was left of it when it cooled, but Brevard County law enforcement knew it was an Explorer, and that Orange County officials were looking for one.

By occupation, John Huggins was a landscaper, but he never seemed to have work. Crime, he had discovered, was more lucrative than stoop labor.

Huggins had a long rap sheet, a violent temper, and a reputation for violence against women. As the investigation into Carla Larson's death continued, Huggins's name kept popping up. One witness described a man matching Huggins's general description driving a white Explorer from some undeveloped property in the vicinity of where Carla Larson's body was discovered. The information Angel had provided was certainly helpful, and the burned-out shell of the Explorer, which had last been seen in Brevard County, added to the growing mound of information, but the authorities still needed more evidence.

The police got the break they were looking for when they searched the home of Faye Elms, Angel Huggins's mother, in Brevard County. She presented the officers with several pieces of jewelry that Carla Larson had worn on June 10, which Faye had found hidden in an electrical box in an outbuilding on the property. The sheriff's deputies took the jewelry back to Orlando and showed it to Jim Larson, whose eyes welled up with tears up when he saw the pieces. They were his wife's, he told them. Detectives also took the jewelry to a lab in North Carolina for DNA testing.

On August 20, 1997, the Orange County grand jury returned an indictment for murder for John Huggins. On January 25, 1999, jury selection began in Jacksonville. The trial began several days later. The state presented the jurors with a meticulous, thorough, but circumstantial case. The jury, composed of nine women and three men, deliberated for four hours before returning guilty verdicts on all counts. A week later, the jury heard the sentencing phase. Jim Larson spoke on behalf of himself and the couple's daughter, who would grow up without her mother. Carla's mother, Phyllis Thomas, also addressed the jurors. The state asked for the death penalty; the defense team, lawyers Robert Wesley and Tyrone King, lobbied for life imprisonment. The jurors deliberated for more than two hours and returned to recommend, by a vote of eight to four, that Huggins receive the death penalty. Judge Belvin Perry set a sentencing date of February 26, 1999.

Sentencing took place in the Orange County courthouse, and to the surprise of no one, John Steven Huggins was sentenced to death.

In Florida, a death sentence ends the trial phase for the accused but springs a lengthy appeals process into action. Huggins's appeals process had barely gotten under way when a citizen approached one of the defense attorneys and informed him that he had seen a woman strongly resembling Angel Huggins driving a Ford Explorer on International Drive, the main tourist drag in Orlando, the day after Carla Larson's disappearance. The allegation, if verified, would call Angel Huggins's testimony into question. The prosecutors and defense team disagreed over the state's handling of the information, and the defense turned the matter over to Judge Perry, who ruled that the state had withheld exculpatory evidence from the defense and threw out Huggins's conviction.

Osceola County was selected as the site for Huggins's second murder trial, but too many people remembered the tale of the young mother strangled to death in next-door Orange County, and the trial required another new venue. Tampa, seat of Hillsborough County, was selected as the site. Judge Perry gaveled the start of the trial on July 15, 2002. The defense had a new witness in the man who saw the woman resembling Angel Huggins at the wheel, but the prosecution had two new witnesses come forward. One was a young man who worked as an electrical specialist and knew Carla Larson. He had seen her just before lunchtime on June 10, and later in the afternoon he saw a man resembling John Huggins driving a vehicle resembling Larson's out of the woods onto the eastbound lane of the Osceola Parkway, near where her body was found. The other witness was a Brevard County woman who saw John Huggins driving a Ford Explorer covered with a clumsily applied coat of black spray paint near her home in Eau Gallie.

The second trial was not without a few startling moments, none more so than when, on the day final arguments ceased, Huggins asked the judge to dismiss his attorneys and allow him to represent himself. Judge Perry granted Huggins's wish but ordered his attorneys to support him as advisors. Then the jurors deliberated in this second trial and, after five hours in the jury room, returned with a second guilty verdict.

A day later, Huggins again learned his fate: death.

John Huggins was no stranger to crime. But the murder of Carla Larson was a first for him, and after the second conviction, he seemed to better understand the gravity of what he had been convicted of and what could happen as a result. As a criminal, Huggins tried to conceal the evidence of his deeds, and as a convicted murderer on death row, he seemed equally zealous in disrupting the state's case against him, putting it off its mission of carrying out his execution.

In 2006, Judge Perry weighed the counsel of several physicians who advised him that Huggins was incompetent and unable to assist with his defense. In late 2009, the judge again ruled him competent, but by the summer of 2010, the tables had turned again, when a psychologist ruled that Huggins was again exhibiting symptoms of mental illness. Judge Perry ordered more evaluations, but Huggins refused to cooperate with the physicians assigned to do the evaluation. He also refused to work with his defense team.

John Steven Huggins seems determined to wring out every last moment of time he has left.

CHAPTER 12

2003: A Fantasy Island Murder

Fred Keller, who had been born Fred Bohlander, was the poster boy for the transformative powers of Palm Beach, a place not always jokingly referred to as Fantasy Island.

Keller first came to Palm Beach County in 1957, and like many people, he looked across the Intracoastal Waterway to the lights glittering on Palm Beach with a mixture of wistfulness, envy, and indignation, wanting to be among the "haves" who frolicked there, living the good life, playing, and partying like—and with—rock stars.

A worker in the construction industry at the time, Bohlander promised himself he'd someday become one of Palm Beach's landed gentry, live in a grand mansion, and enjoy the good life in the exclusive enclave. Many people make similar vows to themselves, but Fred Keller actually made it happen.

The son of a German carpenter and a homemaker who immigrated to New York in the early 1930s, Bohlander grew up in a home that lionized the Aryan model of superiority. Young Fred had been told from an early age that he was blessed with the right bloodlines and the designer genes to carry on the noble tradition. A proud, arrogant man, he evaluated potential mates with the same cold, detached eye of a farmer eyeing breeding stock—matters of the heart had nothing to do with it.

Fred's first wife, Blanch, had been married once before and had a son named Brian, who Bohlander adopted. In time the union produced two more sons, Eric and Paul. Over time, the marriage soured and after many threats and much abuse, Blanch left. Her husband followed her and snatched the three boys.

Fred changed their names from Bohlander to Keller, and then fled first to Germany, then to Spain. He finally returned to the United States, settling in Arlington, Virginia. Brian was sent to a foster home to live while Keller's two biological sons remained with him. Keller's parents moved from Long Island to help him raise the boys.

Fred had shown himself to be uncommonly adroit at buying and selling commercial and industrial properties. He could spot bargains and flip the properties quickly, fetching maximum profit in minimal time. His success in the venture turned quickly to wealth, and Keller built on it rapidly. In 1984, he finally made good on his promise to himself and moved to Palm Beach.

Keller was not having as much success in his personal life. Three more marriages had gone sour for him. Affairs of the heart had never been easy for Keller, who liked his wives exceptionally younger than him, beautiful, submissive, and doting.

On Palm Beach, women occupy a powerful and symbolic role. They are the movers and shakers behind the considerable social life of the island, and the right wife with the right connections enhances the power and virility of a man. Keller wanted a woman in his life who would make other men envious, and serve as arm candy for public appearances—although Palm Beach's famed charity balls were not his concern. Keller wasn't into philanthropy; his favorite cause was himself.

Much like the fisherman who decides to switch to a new fishing spot after having no luck in one, Keller decided to change his hunt for the perfect wife. He reasoned he'd been unsuccessful in large measure because he had selected unworthy or inferior women from the available pool of American women, who were far too aggressive and not appreciative enough for his tastes anyway, So Keller tried a different tack and asked his relatives to place an ad in German newspapers for his next wife.

The ad lured several possible candidates and one prize catch— a lovely auburn-haired model with delicate features from a small town outside Dusseldorf. Her name was Rosemarie Keil, and in 1992 she became the fifth Mrs. Fred Keller.

Not long after Rose's arrival, Keller was diagnosed with leukemia, but a new wife thirty-five years younger than he and the promise of a more exciting life gave him the spirit to fight the disease. He even had surgery to reverse a vasectomy so he could father a child. Not long afterward, Rose gave birth to another Keller heir, a blond-haired son he named Fred Jr., but lovingly called Fredchen.

Despite her delicate beauty, Rose Keller was no wilting flower. Soft-spoken but not shy, she was neither feckless nor some vapid little thing; instead, she was a quick study of her husband. She showed over time she had become as shrewd and ruthless as the man she married.

Rose's hard edge was one thing; Fred's rough edges were quite unique. He lived like a prince in his castle on the north end of Palm Beach, but he conducted his day-to-day life as though he were a pauper. Palm Beach is known for its glitzy, glittering balls and other social events, but Fred made sure the Kellers took no part in the social life of the island. In an area where conspicuous consumption is the norm, Keller wore clothes and shoes until they faded, became threadbare, and developed holes. He drove around the island in rattletrap vehicles and furnished the office of the Keller Trust Company with garish carpet, cheap paneling, and mismatched furniture. Keller was fond of filing lawsuits over the most trivial matters and piddling amounts. He once sued one of his sons and a girlfriend for whom he had bought silicone breast implants. Whether over a business deal gone bad or some other perceived slight, Fred couldn't stand losing and sought retribution any way he could accomplish it.

Rose correctly suspected Fred's assets were phenomenal and insisted on taking a role in the Keller Trust Company. Fred allowed her a little access to placate her. Finally, she insisted that since she had helped build the company's assets, she should become an equal partner in its spoils. That's where Fred dug in his heels. In 2000, Rose filed for divorce.

There was no such thing as a simple transaction with Fred Keller, particularly when attorneys were involved, and it was clear to Rose that to prevail in the divorce, she'd have to hunker down and prepare for a long, hard struggle. In 2001, though, Fred nearly died of leukemia, and Rose was there for him, lovingly ministering to his needs throughout the ordeal. When his disease went into remission, the divorce proceedings lumbered forward again. Few Palm Beach divorces are uncomplicated, but the Keller divorce was exceptionally messy and convoluted. Both sides were interested in demonizing the other as part of their strategy, plus there were a variety of legal issues to sort through, such as a prenuptial agreement to be challenged, Fredchen's custody and visitation issues, and the equitable division of the financial assets of the marriage.

The judge in the case ruled that Rose was entitled to half of the marital assets, making her a very wealthy woman. The decision didn't make clear, however, that the divorce was final, so attorneys ramped up for another round of motions, hearings, and appeals to deal with that potentially thorny legal omission. It was still apparent, however, that Rose would emerge from the ordeal as a very rich woman.

On the morning of November 10, 2003, Fred and Rose were to begin the actual process of dividing the marital assets. Rose, joined by her brother Wolfgang Keil, met with Keller at the Riviera Beach offices of Keller Trust. Rose and her brother were escorted into Keller's private office, where Keller placed papers before Keil, who served as his sister's very capable advisor. As Keil studied the papers, Keller turned his back and reached for his briefcase. Moments later, shots rang out.

When Keller Trust staff heard the noise, they summoned help. When police and paramedics broke into the room, they found Rose dead on the floor with a single gunshot to the head. Wolfgang Keil had been shot three times, but was still alive. Fred Keller had been shot once, in the left cheek.

As details emerged from the forensic evidence and interviews of Keil and Keller, Keller was charged with murdering Rose and wounding Keil. Fred's injury had come about as a result of Keil and Keller struggling over the gun and a shot being discharged as a result.

At his trial, Keller's attorney suggested a different scenario, one that blamed Keil for having made a threatening move toward Keller and pulling out an object Keller thought was a pistol, but was instead a cellular phone. Keller responded by pulling out his gun, but it was Keil, Keller asserted, who accidentally shot his sister in the scuffle. Keller's first trial ended in a hung jury. The second trial ended in conviction on both counts, and Keller was sentenced to two life terms plus fifteen years.

Three months after his sentencing. Fred was transferred to the South Florida Reception Center south of Miami in preparation for his transfer to prison, but his leukemia had resurfaced and his health faltered badly. He was taken to the Larkin Community Hospital, where he died on August 23, 2007. One of his attorneys was at his bedside when he passed away.

Fred Keller's body was transported back from Miami-Dade to Palm Beach County for cremation and disposal, but before that could happen, Wolfgang Keil asked for permission to view Keller's lifeless corpse to ease his mind and bring closure. Keil also wanted to bring Fredchen, age twelve at the time, to the funeral home to see his father one last time. Fredchen was Fred Keller's sole heir; Keller's two other biological sons had died earlier. As had become customary in the family, a corps of lawyers dealt with the request by taking it to court. The judge ruled that Keil had no authority in determining who viewed the body.

Legal wrangling over the Keller estate has significantly reduced its size from the $100 million it was originally estimated to be worth. The Keller mansion on North Lake Way was razed and the land that looked over the Intracoastal Waterway sold as two separate pieces for a record-low price of $3.675 million. Keller's personal effects, from pieces of art such as a pair of Asian foo dog sculptures, to kitsch and assorted personal household items, were sold in a two-hundred-item estate sale that raised a very modest sum of about $50,000.

Acknowledgments

Catherine Cole dedicates this book to the following people:

To Pam Lower and Susan Ferguson—I never would have made it through the last two years without you both. Thanks for always being on the other end of a phone, no matter the time.

And to Madeline Grace Lower—my sweet baby. In your short life, you have dealt with more than your fair share and have taught me so much. I love you to the moon and back!

And to Cindy Young—for teaching me nearly everything MGL has not. From my first professional newspaper story to our first book, you have been an incredible editor, mentor, coach, and most importantly, friend. You are the best, Cindy. Thanks from the bottom of my heart.

And to Levi, Rylan, and Dexter Cole—I finally have the "sons" I always wanted. Thanks for letting me share your dad. Oh, and, POKE!

And, finally, to Jeff Cole—thanks for making everything fun. You ROCK.

Cynthia Young dedicates this book to the following people:

To my mom, Robbie, because all goodness springs from somewhere, and I've come to learn that whatever of it I possess comes from you. To my brother Joe, who helps give me perspective; my husband Jim, who helps me keep my priorities straight and to the light of my life, Nicholas, who keeps me thinking, laughing and makes me a better person. I love and cherish you all.

And to Cathy Cole, my former *Sun-Tattler* colleague who became a most excellent writing partner, muse and a friend of unparalleled quality. I knew from the moment I met you that I wanted to be your friend. I want to grow up to be the kind of person you are.

The authors give special thanks to Audra Shaneman, communications specialist, Mariner Sands Country Club, Stuart.

Bibliography

Books

Bishop, Jim. *The Murder Trial of Judge Peel.* New York: Simon and Schuster, 1962.

Burnett, Gene M. *Florida's Past: People & Events That Shaped the State.* Vol. 2. Sarasota, FL: Pineapple Press, 1988.

Cavaioli, Frank J. *Pompano Beach: A History.* Charleston, SC: The History Press, 2007.

Huffstodt, James T. *Everglades Lawmen: True Stories of Game Wardens in the Glades.* Sarasota, FL: Pineapple Press, 2000.

Indiana, Gary. *Three Month Fever: The Andrew Cunanan Story.* New York: Cliff Street Books/HarperCollins Publishers, 1999.

Jessica Lunsford Act. Florida Department of Education Technical Paper. August 2005.

Kleinberg, Eliot. *Wicked Palm Beach: Lifestyles of the Rich and Heinous.* Charleston, SC: The History Press, 2009.

Leamer, Lawrence. *Madness under the Royal Palms.* New York: Hyperion Books, 2009.

Logan, Richard, and Tere Duperrault Fassbender. *Alone: Orphaned on the Ocean.* Green Bay, WI: TitleTown Publishing, 2010.

McIver, Stuart B. "The Good Ol' Ashley Boys." *Murder in the Tropics: The Florida Chronicles.* Vol. 2. Sarasota, FL: Pineapple Press, 1995.

———. "The Island City." Wilton Manors, FL: City of Wilton Manors, 1997.

———. "The Sea Waif's Story." *Murder in the Tropics: The Florida Chronicles.* Vol. 2. Sarasota, FL: Pineapple Press, 1995.

———. "Judgement Day." *Murder in the Tropics: The Florida Chronicles.* Vol. 2. Sarasota, FL: Pineapple Press, 1995.

Nash, Robert Jay. *The Great Pictorial History of World Crime.* Vol. 2. Wilmette, IL: History Inc., 2004.

Russell, Sue. *Lethal Intent.* New York: Kensington, 2002.

Simmons, Glen, and Laura Ogden. *Gladesmen: Gator Hunters, Moonshiners and Skiffers.* Gainesville: University Press of Florida, 1998.

Wilbanks, William. *Forgotten Heroes: Police Officers Killed in Early Florida, 1840–1925.* Nashville, TN: Turner, 1998.

Williams, Ada Coats. *Florida's Ashley Gang.* Port Salerno, FL: Florida Classics Library, 1996.

Newspapers, Magazines, and Other Periodicals

Baker, Donald P., and Audrey Gillan. "Police Check if Cunanan Had Help," *Washington Post*, July 25, 1997: A1.

Bogert, John "The tale of the *Bluebelle* still captivates decades later," *The (Torrance, CA) Daily Breeze*, May 26, 2010.

Bragg, Rick. "Living with a Grief That Will Never Die, after the Murders of 2 Loved Ones." *New York Times*, March 22, 1999.

Bumpus-Hooper, Lynn, and Laurin Sellers, "Schwab guilty in death of Junny Rios-Martinez," *Orlando Sentinel*, May 23, 1992.

Bumpus-Hooper, Lynn, "Senate OKs longer jail times for rapists," *Orlando Sentinel*, June 26, 1992.

———. "Hunt for Boy Leads to [*sic*] Ohio Police to Question Schwab—Junny Still Missing." *Orlando Sentinel*, April 22, 1991.

"Carlie's Crusade teaches Milton students self-defense techniques," *Poughkepsie (NY) Journal*, March 21, 2008.

"Coast Guard rules Bluebelle ketch was intentionally sunk," *Greeley (CO) Tribune*, April 25, 1962.

Colarossi, Anthony. "John Huggins: Killer Had Delusions about Feds, Mafia, Psychologist Says." *Orlando Sentinel*, July 15, 2010.

———. "Judge Sets Special Meeting with Death Row Inmate John Huggins." *Orlando Sentinel*, October 8, 2010.

"Convicted Child Killer John Evander Couey Dies in Prison, before Planned Execution," *New York Daily News*, October 1, 2009.

Cooper, Meryl, "Chillingworth Memorial Scholarship," *Florida State Times*, September 2000.

"Court to write next chapter on 'Bluebelle,'" *The (Hendersonville, NC) Times-News*, April 17, 1962.

Crumbo, Chuck. "Unearthed Skull Is Linked to Suspected Mass Killer," *Fort Lauderdale News and Sun-Sentinel*, May 13, 1978: 1, 5A.

Dargan, Michele, "Fred Keller estate attorneys battle in court over fees, how much money remains for son," *Palm Beach Daily News*, May 13, 2010.

———, "In second trial, Keller convicted of killing ex-wife, wounding her brother," *Palm Beach Daily News*, Feb. 1, 2007.

———, "The decade: Fred Keller convicted of killing ex-wife Rosemarie, but case took years in courts," *Palm Beach Daily News*, December 26, 2009.

Decker, Twila. "Double-Crossed by Death," *St. Petersburg Times*, February 24, 1999.

"Deputy Sheriff Hendrickson shot down in cold blood, Bob Ashley, the murderer, shot and will not live," *Miami Metropolis*, June 2, 1915.

Diaz, Missy, "Retrial soon in murder case," *South Florida Sun-Sentinel*, Jan. 8, 2007.

———, "Victim wants to end doubts," *South Florida Sun-Sentinel*, August 28, 2007.

Florida Department of Corrections. "Inmate John Evander Couey Dies of Natural Causes; Was on Death Row for Murder of Jessica Lunsford." Press release, September 30, 2009.

"Follow up: Junny Rios-Martinez," *Orlando Sentinel*, Sept. 29, 1993.

Frank, John, "Five years after Jessica Lunsford's killing, legislators rethink sex offender laws," *St. Petersburg Times*, Feb. 24, 2010.

Fretland, Katie, and Willoughby Mariano. "Police Close 1966 Mystery," *Orlando Sentinel*, July 18, 2007.

Gerds, Warren, "Orphan's tale to air on TV in Japan," *Green Bay Press-Gazette*, August 2, 2010.

Glover, Scott. "Death Puts End to Trial of Suspected Serial Killer," *South Florida Sun-Sentinel*, December 5, 1995.

Glover, Scott, and Jaime Abdo. "Untangling Tortured Web of a Killer," *South Florida Sun-Sentinel*, December 13, 1995.

Holsman, Melissa E. "Evidence in St. Lucie County Museum of Murder Helped Put Away Church Arsonist, Serial Killer," *Stuart News*, November 19, 2010.

"Hot Water Possible Cause of Deadly Fight," *South Florida Sun-Sentinel*, February 3, 1996.

"Indictment names Joseph A. Peel, Jr., others," *Securities and Exchange Commission News Digest*, June 20, 1961: 4.

Kacoha, Margie, "Possessions of Fred Keller, convicted murderer, garner about $50K at estate auction," *Palm Beach Daily News*, Dec. 6, 2008.

"Kin Tell Plan for Terry Jo," *The Milwaukee Journal*, November 29, 1961: 14.

Kleinberg, Howard, "Ashley gang a Florida terror," *The Miami News*, Sept. 18, 1982: 4B.

Kroening, Leigh Ann Wagner, "Kewaunee woman's book details family's murder and the aftermath," *Green Bay Press-Gazette/Kewaunee County News*, June 23, 2010.

Lesley, Elena, "Jessie's Riders tell Couey to beware," *St. Petersburg Times*, February 24, 2007.

Lundy, Sarah, "11-year-old victim's parents see child killer die," *Orlando Sentinel*, July 2, 2008.

Lush, Tamara, "The millionaire, model, and gun," *St. Petersburg Times*, Feb. 9, 2005.

Mattise, Jonathan. "Panel Recalls Serial Killer Gerard Schaefer Whose Victims Ended Up on Hutchinson Island," *Stuart News*, April 27, 2009.

Mayhew, Augustus. "Lakefront Palm Beach lot of convicted murderer Fred Keller sells for $3.675 million," *Palm Beach Daily News*, July 29, 2009.

Medaris, Michael. "Jimmy Ryce Law Enforcement Training Center Program." *Office of Juvenile Justice and Delinquency Prevention Newsletter*. Fact Sheet 62. March 1997.

Mullikin, James. "The Homicidal Rampage of Mr. Clean." *True Police Cases*, April 1974: 13, 14, 64-65.

"Murderer of Desoto Tiger Being Traced," *Miami Metropolis*, January 8, 1912.

Musgrave, Jane, "State supreme court suspends West Palm Beach attorney after clients' money disappears," *The Palm Beach Post*, March 25, 2009.

————, "West Palm Beach attorney Clark Cone charged with stealing from clients," *The Palm Beach Post*, August 26, 2009.

————, "Lawyer's fall stirs gruesome memories," *The Palm Beach Post*, Sept. 26, 2009: 1, 14A.

Nagy, John A. "Sex-Offender Bill Faces Legislative Clock," *Florida Today*, March 10, 1992, 2B.

Nolin, Robert. "Two 1966 Deaths Linked to Convicted Killer," *South Florida Sun-Sentinel*, July 19, 2007.

Orth, Maureen. "The Killer's Trail." *Vanity Fair*, September 1997.

Presley, Mari M., "Jimmy Ryce Involuntary Civil Commitment for Sexually Violent Predators Treatment and Care Act: Replacing Criminal Justice with Civil Commitment," *Florida State University Law Review*, 1999.

Robles, Frances, John Lantigua, and Martin Merzer. "Police Confirm It Was Cunanan's Body in the Houseboat," *Miami Herald*, July 24, 1997.

Roen, Samuel. *Evidence of Murder: A Twisted Killer's Trail of Violence*. New York: Pinnacle Books, 2003.

"Ruling is reserved in Holzapfel case," *St. Petersburg Times*, June 13, 1970: 3B.

Sedensky, Matt. "Versace House Tour, Overnight Stays, Come with Hefty Price Tags," *Knoxville (TN) News Sentinel*, December 28, 2008.

Sellers, Laurin, and Lynne Bumpus-Hooper. "Schwab's Letter Describes Killer Suspect: Donald Killed Junny but 'No One Believes' It," *Orlando Sentinel*, May 14, 1991.

"Slaying of Ashley Gang ends long crime career," *Miami Daily News*, Nov. 3, 1924.

Solomon, Scott. "Junny's Parents Reject Plea Offer," *Florida Today*, May 16, 1992.

Sonne, Warren, "The Ashley Gang: What *Really* Happened?" *Indian River Magazine*, October 2007.

Tisch, Chris. "State Executes Child Killer," *St. Petersburg Times*, July 2, 2008.

Taylor, Jill. "Former Public Defender Marks 50 Years," *Palm Beach Post*, June 27, 2004.

"The King and Queen of the Everglades," *Historic Okeechobee*, undated newsletter: 1, 14.

"The Scoutmaster and the Judge," *Time*, November 14, 1960.

Thorbahn, Carl, "Holzapfel case rests; Judge Chillingworth 'watches' hearing," *Palm Beach Post*, June 13, 1970: B1.

Torres, John A. "Child Killer's Final Hours Tick Away in Florida's First Execution in 18 Months," *Palm Beach Post*, July 1, 2008.

Turner, Jim, "Stuart restaurant in old Ashley Gang target closes after owners can't make the rent," *Stuart News*, September 17, 2009.

Vansickle, Abbie, and Justin George. "Was Jessica Lunsford a Captive for 3 Days?" *St. Petersburg Times*, May 27, 2005.

Vincent, Lynn. "Death penalty on Ice," *World Magazine*, December 1, 2007.

Websites

www.amw.com/fugitives/case.cfm?id=39789

www.answers.com/topic/ted-bundy

www.associatedcontent.com

www.biography.com/articles/Ted-Bundy-9231165

www.biography.com/notorious/crimefiles.do?catId=259456&action=view& profileId=262833

www.carpenoctem.tv/killers/wournos.html

www.cbsnews.com/stories/2004/07/23/national/main631473.shtml

www.ccadp.org/aileenwuornos.htm

www.charleyproject.org

www.clickorlando.com/news/817364/detail.html

www.coralgables.com

http://crime.about.com/od/serial/p/tedbundy.htm

http://crime.about.com/od/serial/p/tedbundy2.htm

www.crime-safety-security.com/Verbal-Self-Defense.html

www.crimescene.com

www.danny-rolling.blogspot.com

www.dep.state.fl.us/gwt.guide

http://foia.fbi.gov/foiaindex/bundy.htm

www.gainesville.com

www.greenbayhub.greenbaypressgazette.com

www.gwinnetforum.com

www.heraldtribune.com

http://hubpages.com/hub/Ted_Bundy

www.huffingtonpost.com/2008/12/16/adam-walsh-kille _151464.html

www.ir.ufl.edu

http://lesbianlife.about.com/cs/famouslesbians/p/AileenW

www.lindseywilliams.org

http://magazine.ufl.edu/2010/10/we-remember/

www.mayhem.net
www.missingkids.com
www.monstropedia.org/index.php?title=Ottis_Toole
www.msnbc.msn.com/id/28257294/
www.ncsl.org
http://network.nationalpost.com/np/blogs/posted/archive/2008/12/16/who-was
   -ottis-toole.aspx www.nickbroomfield.com
http://nixonfoundation.org
www.orlandosentinel.com
www.oprah.com
www.president.ufl.edu/pastPres/lombardi.htm
www.quazen.com/.../10-weird-facts-about-ted-bundys-childhood/
www.serialkillerdatabase.com
www.skcentral.com/articles.php?article_id=525
www.themacklecompany.com
www.tldm.org/news6/bundy.htm
www.trutv.com
www.uff.ufl.edu/Scholarships/ScholarshipInfo.asp?ScholarshipFund=004031
www.waterwayguide.com